Penguin Books

the Olive Grove

Patrice Newell was born in Adelaide in 1956 and
now lives in Gundy, New South Wales.

PATRICE NEWELL

the Olive Grove

PENGUIN BOOKS

Penguin Books Australia Ltd
487 Maroondah Highway, PO Box 257
Ringwood, Victoria 3134, Australia
Penguin Books Ltd
Harmondsworth, Middlesex, England
Penguin Putnam Inc.
375 Hudson Street, New York, New York 10014, USA
Penguin Books Canada Limited
10 Alcorn Avenue, Toronto, Ontario, Canada M4V 3B2
Penguin Books (NZ) Ltd
Cnr Rosedale and Airborne Roads, Albany, Auckland, New Zealand
Penguin Books (South Africa) (Pty) Ltd
5 Watkins Street, Denver Ext 4, 2094, South Africa
Penguin Books India (P) Ltd
11, Community Centre, Panchsheel Park, New Delhi 110 017, India

First published by Penguin Books Australia Ltd 2000

10 9 8 7

Designed by Nikki Townsend, Penguin Design Studio
Typeset in Berkeley Book by Post Pre-press Group, Brisbane, Queensland
Printed in Australia by Australian Print Group, Maryborough, Victoria

National Library of Australia
Cataloguing-in-Publication data:

Newell, Patrice, 1956– .
    The olive grove.

ISBN 0 14 029868 1.

1. Newell, Patrice, 1956– . 2. Women farmers – New South Wales – Upper Hunter
Region – Biography. 3. Organic farming – New South Wales – Upper Hunter Region.
4. Olive industry and trade – New South Wales – Upper Hunter Region.
I. Title.

630.92

This project has been assisted by the Commonwealth Government
through the Australia Council, its arts funding and advisory body.

www.penguin.com.au

In memory of
Thelma Anne Newell (1914–1999)
Felix Leslie Newell (1919–1986)

We say it is time to stop assuming that discoveries only move us forward. The war against nature has to end. And we are going to stop it.

Lord Peter Melchett,
organic farmer, Executive Director of Greenpeace UK

How did this happen?

It's 1986 and my father is dying. At best he has a few months to live. Most weekends Phillip and I drive from Sydney to Adelaide to see him, from my new home town to my old, a 1500-kilometre round trip. It would be easier to fly but I need these long journeys locked in a moving car with an everchanging backdrop.

My map tears along the crease marks, the edges smudge where I write important notes: the names of quiet motels, where a decent coffee can be had at Balranald, a petrol station with clean toilets. We become familiar with places I'd never heard of and begin to notice the progress of crops, different coloured soils, types of trees, the vastness of dull plains. We admire the ancient river gums along the Murray's edge, the beauty of peaceful towns nestled behind hills. The mountains, lakes, gullies and wetlands twist and turn my mood.

We are calm in the car. The landscape makes no demands this way. For seven months this is our routine. Until finally, bravely, Dad dies.

Slowly, without noticing the change, we realise we need to be out of the car rather than in it. To be part of the landscape rather than passing through it. So we begin to read real estate ads for rural properties.

I've had enough disappointment this year. Let's not set unattainable goals. I want the pleasure of looking to linger. We visit a few houses on blocks of 2 or 4 hectares. We speak to friends on the land. A casual hunt begins. We'll know, I say, when we find the right place. We just will. It is after all a folly of an idea. We work in the city and need all that gorgeous Sydney can provide. I rely on its energy when I wilt. What would I do anyway, out there?

People dream about owning a place that truly reflects who they are or who they'd like to be. While I had dreams, they were dreams I never believed I'd fulfil. Consequently, I hadn't been disappointed as I moved from flat to flat with carloads of disposable possessions. But not next time for me.

I grew up in a nondescript suburb called Kurralta Park where, despite my mother's efforts at housekeeping, our dilapidated brick house would never be socially acceptable because it was back to front. Open our front door and you'd see the fridge, the sink and the stove. Open the back door and there was the copper and clothes wringer. We greeted passers-by while we washed the dishes. I played more in the front yard than the back. Our life was public.

We were part of the working class I heard about on the news. Yet it wasn't a poor life. It was simple, and without decoration, but rich in freedom, safety, love, community. I didn't appreciate then that Dad earned so little sorting mail at the General Post Office, or that Mum struggled to pay for my gym lessons and school excursions by cleaning offices and, later, making shoes in a factory. Complaining was never tolerated in our half Catholic, half Anglican house. 'Be grateful for what you've got,' Dad always said somewhat defensively.

I had a full Catholic education because, as my mother tried to explain, 'I think it's good having the Virgin Mary as a role model.' What? Why? Years later, when we travelled through Italy, she was connected to all the great art through the holy pictures I'd brought home as a school kid. The same ones I now buy for my little girl Aurora, whom we call Rory, to use as book marks in her A.A Milne and *Tintin* books. Such a natural introduction to Raphael and Giotto.

One afternoon, standing erect and sweltering in the St Joseph's Primary School yard at assembly, I heard Sister William, looking uncannily like Mary MacKillop, blasting out over the speakers. 'Do you know what you're meant to learn here at school?' Hers was a voice of certainty. A few ideas flickered through my sun-bleached brain: Jesus is the son of God, the Virgin Mary's my protector, the times table, how to read. But I didn't need to guess, because Sister William was busting to tell us the answer. 'You're here to learn about *life*. It doesn't matter about passing tests,' she continued (how many principals would say that today?), 'or if your team wins. Now is the time to learn about what really matters, to learn right from wrong.'

She went on to use words I was unsure of, but afterwards, in the shade, a few of us talked about what a moral imperative might be and wondered if any of us could ever be as certain about ours as Sister William was of hers.

The themes at Kurralta Park were maintained at St Aloysius College during high school, where the Mercy nuns seemed even more politically engaged. Certainly the lay teachers chosen to work with the nuns were an eccentric bunch, incorporating social causes in the lessons: Aboriginal health, women in science, family planning. Looking back, it is the discussions between the classes that I remember most, the way a phrase lodges in the imagination, how a new word gives sudden clarity. Though not a particularly successful student, I was never worried by it. Sister William's declaration to this seven- or eight-year-old has resonated ever since.

At thirteen I sat on the kitchen step knowing, with a deep certainty, that as soon as I could I was leaving. The whole world awaited, and Kurralta Park just wasn't gonna do. And I did go. My big plan was to train as a nurse at Darwin, but Cyclone Tracy put an end to that by flattening the hospital. As I waited in Adelaide for the hospital to be rebuilt and for my training to begin, I accepted more and more modelling work. I posed in underwear for John Martin catalogues, I simpered over bottles of detergent, I jumped out of sports cars waving brightly for the Bank of South Australia, now defunct. Then unexpectedly, after an inconsequential suburban fashion parade, an agent from Sydney offered to represent me. I couldn't wait to pack and get on a plane.

But I didn't stop in Sydney. From the age of eighteen, I moved to countless places, settling in Melbourne, Guam, Manila, Bacolod, New York, Chicago – modelling, waitressing, promoting products I'm too embarrassed to remember, and conducting low-rent celebrity interviews for magazines. Until finally, after a wedding at Niagara Falls to Cameron, a composer, I found myself in a flat we'd decked out in black leather and chrome in Kings Cross. And stashed in a box high in the back of a wardrobe were old clothes I was keeping for the day I could afford to move to a farm.

Seven years passed. At some point in time, and I don't know who did it, the clothes were thrown out. Along with the dream.

A cover shot for *Good Housekeeping* marked the end of my modelling career. Had I realised I was saying goodbye to being a clothes horse, I would have insisted on champagne. In a case of who you know paying off, I was offered a job as a television researcher for the news department. Though earning a quarter of my usual income, I looked forward to going to work. But this behind-the-scenes job at Channel 7 didn't last long. Two years later I was back in front of the camera, reporting, reading news, painting on lipstick and thinking too much about what I was wearing.

This life, so manic and anxious, a combination of glamour and squalor, brought on the first of my mid-life crises. My friends in their twenties formed a community of the tired, the frustrated, the disappointed, the envious and the world-weary. We asked world-weary questions: What's it all about? Why am I doing this? Do I really hate my job? Am I happy? Do I like my friends? And we gave world-weary answers.

I was jolted out of my self-indulgence by the news of my father's illness and the Kurralta Park motto ringing loudly in my head. Be grateful for your lot, or, to put it another way, stop bloody whingeing. Only by the grace of God did you miss out on pimples and not turn out fat, ugly, sick and dumb. Get perspective, girl.

But I rejected that advice and changed everything. Quickly, almost carelessly. I bought my own flat. I left my husband. I ended a second career in television. And I began life with Phillip Adams, a father of three daughters and seventeen years my senior.

At the age of thirty, having travelled the world many times over, I settled on a farm called Elmswood, near a little town called Gundy, near a larger town called Scone, in the Upper Hunter Valley in the state of New South Wales.

'You must be mad!' my dear friend Paula the makeup artist says when she hears of my plans. Then adds as an after-thought, 'It's a long holiday really, isn't it? I mean, Patrice, seriously, what would you do up there?' Sal, a fellow reporter says, 'How can you move to a district that elects a National Party bastard to parliament?' John, a television producer, patronises, 'What a waste.'

Living in the country, *wasteful*?

You see, real people don't move to the country. The pre-vailing view is that the country, like Adelaide, is a place to leave, not to live in. At best the country is a place you visit. Preferably on weekends. Urbanites consider farming a dog's job or a tax dodge. Oh yes, there's serious agribusiness, those mechanised, monocultural rural enterprises managed from town where profits go to a corporation, usually over-seas. But that's not the farming I want to do, which involves the desire to really work the land – where you're dust-covered or mud-splattered, depending on the season; working as a mechanic, a water expert, a weight lifter, a soil analyst, all before smoko.

I'd been working with people who lived to be *seen*. Watching each other, watching themselves, being watched.

Theirs is the postmodern world. Out here, around the hills of Gundy, no one is watching. No one sees me reverse from the garage in a four-wheel drive to drive to a gully with a pile of books, intent on identifying an unusual grass. Nobody is watching when I get up at dawn to help cut testes from young calves, or butcher a lamb on the kitchen table with a bandsaw. Only I see, and the experience is liberating. I sing everywhere I go.

In Sydney I wouldn't walk half a block to the deli unless I felt I looked reasonably intact, now I walk for miles not giving a stuff. I don't worry about my hair, I forget to put on deodorant, my shirt is torn, my boots smeared with cow dung. After sixteen years of plucking, waxing, brushing, and patting, it doesn't matter any more. Oh, the joys of a mirrorless life!

I was fourteen when I began earning pocket money from modelling. Photo shoots before school, those shopping-mall fashion parades on weekends. Even television journalism is as much about makeup and hairspray as the report. Now, no one is telling me what a good job I've done. No one is patting my back, no publicist is arranging an interview. Soon, no one is saying anything at all. So far I don't miss the false compliments, the insecure fuss. But will I be able to sustain a future without them? Without the city?

Working the land is a calling being stripped of respect. I used to laugh at the cluster of country folk in funny hats when they came to town for the Royal Easter Show. Their concerns were remote and unrecognisable. They lived in a foreign country. Now, when reading about the rural–urban divide, a theme resurrected whenever there's a disaster to report – a drought, flood, fire, suicide, bank closure, or One Nation campaign – I identify with the people on the land. I join them in bemoaning how we are misunderstood, unappreciated and ignored.

I am now a citizen of that foreign country.

Rural life is profoundly domestic. This discovery surprises me. No one told me, or warned me about it. While excited to be unpacking boxes, placing new packets of things on clean shelves, I get tired and want to go down the street for an espresso. That's what I'd normally do, walk out the door for sustenance, conversation, a paper to read. There is no place for a quick fix up here. If you want coffee, you've got to make coffee. You've got to do everything for yourself. And you're a long way from the shops, as I discovered cooking my very first dinner at Elmswood. I found I'd packed pasta but no olive oil, canned tomatoes but no garlic. Worse, I hadn't ordered newspapers or remembered the radio. I felt a deep anxiety. Only one day had passed but already I'd no idea what was going on in the world. Even on overseas holidays – no, more so on holidays – I always remained in touch, seeking out the *Herald Tribune*, devouring every page. Of course there is time in Venice and Cannes to loll about and read. But here at Gundy, I feel completely unconnected to the old world.

A product of my time, I've long regarded my escape from domesticity as a major achievement. Pubescent when Greer wrote *The Female Eunuch*, my generation of women, especially those born in the mid-fifties, thought we were the luckiest of the century: old enough to read such a book but not wise enough to be daunted by the complexities of gender politics. It was a liberating teenagedom.

In growing up I'd moved out of the kitchen. Yet here I was back in it. This could be a serious mistake.

I used to eat at least two meals a day out. That was just something you did. Cooking was what I paid someone else to do. Even when money was tight, there was always enough for coffee and a biscuit at Darlinghurst. My last job in television, as co-host of *The Today Show*, meant a breakfast of bacon and eggs in the canteen before the show's post-mortem. Lunch was with friends, and the evening meal was usually a light snack out of a packet, casually consumed on bed reading over the production notes for the next morning.

I'm not missing television, but I'm missing the casual availability of food. There's a lot of work to be done. Hard, physical work, and I am always hungry. I lose weight. I'm 173 centimetres and down to 52 kilograms. I was never this thin, even when I was modelling. So, urgently, I must learn to cook again. Really cook. Proper food.

Phillip, despite being interested in almost everything, shows a total lack of skill in the kitchen. For him, co-ordinating tea and toast is difficult. He shows amazement at how ingredients combine to feed us. It's not all smooth going, and on discovering the pantry empty a few times Phillip takes over the shopping. It's been full ever since. He doesn't buy one packet of lentils, he buys five. As his mother says, 'You'll have to accept there is one thing Phillip can't do and probably never will and that is cook.' But he can shop.

Still grieving for Dad, my mother moves into a small cottage beside the homestead. Her name is Thelma, we call her place Thelmswood. I walk down to borrow her *Commonsense Cookery Book*, the stained paperback she'd used to teach a thirteen-year-old dreaming of escape. Now that I've escaped I need the book more than ever.

My menu grows. Potato pie, pea and ham soup, roast lamb, scones, pancakes, rock cakes, casseroles, fish cakes, kedgeree, all the old boring things from childhood. All the bland food that drove my later addiction to spice. Here, I need this honest, nutritious food like never before. Phillip loves it. More cook books are added to the kitchen shelves.

Hating to admit it, I begin enjoying the hours at the bench, chopping, mashing, mixing, listening to CDs. I put on weight, regain some stamina, feel I'm coping. My kitchen becomes my local coffee shop, bistro, five-star restaurant, occasional office, meeting place, and eventually a craft room and toyland. Cooking is the new romance, writes a conservative friend from Long Island, now married to a wealthy gynaecologist. Am I letting down the sisterhood?

When I see the chisel plough being dragged across a field, that's business. When I dig the tynes of my gardening fork into the soil alongside the old blacksmith's shed to prepare a new vegie garden, that's living. Planting oats for cattle to eat during winter is essential, but planting food for us to eat is profound.

The vegetable garden transforms the cooking ritual. Within weeks it is productive and has been ever since. How can people live in the country without growing vegetables? Many do, trying once or twice then giving up. It's not that growing vegetables is so difficult, it's a question of timing. People complain about too many zucchinis in summer or too much silver beet in winter.

Sometimes I think I run a French provincial kitchen. Bread is rising, cakes are baking, casseroles are being prepared after breakfast. Vegetables charcoaled at dinnertime transform the following day's salad. In my kitchen, food is a process, not an event.

At this early stage of our life at Elmswood our manager is Reg, ruddy-faced, softly smiling. Born on a cattle and sheep property up past Ellerston, 60 kilometres north-east of here, Reg has been working in the district all his life. He's a talented horseman who wins ribbons at local camp drafts like a military hero wins medals. Many managers insist on *not* doing certain jobs, but Reg knows that a farm involves a multitude of responsibilities and passes no judgement about the comparative worth of tilling soil for vegetables or mustering cattle for the sale yards.

Reg, his wife Yvonne and their three children, Leanne, Jill and Brad, move into another house on the property. Later they'll move on, but Yvonne, dear Yvonne, remains a trusted friend and helpmate, a woman who embodies all the things that are decent and practical about country women. Yvonne musters on her own huge mobs of cattle in rugged country. She can hit a moving target with a rifle. And when Reg was badly injured by a fat steer in their cattle yards, she dragged him out from beneath its hooves and somehow managed to lift him into a four-wheel drive for the 100-kilometre dash to the hospital. She also oversees my first batches of jams, jellies and pickles, and advising on chook care suggests that any egg older than three days can't be classified as fresh and should be put aside for cakes. She teaches me things I don't want to know. When a cow dies giving birth in a paddock near the homestead, Yvonne says, 'Patrice, don't you want to move it?' I ask, 'How?' She grabs a length of rope from the garage, drives to the death site, ties one end around a hoof, loops the other to the tow bar and heads for the hills. I'm very impressed.

Hunger satisfied, I allocate time to overseeing the restoration of our haunted homestead. Hearing one tale about the Elmswood ghost is amusing, hearing two is tolerable, but hearing dozens makes me suspect that what's really haunted are neighbours' imaginations.

As the story goes, and the first part of it turns out to be true, one of the past owners committed suicide by putting a rope around his neck and jumping off the wrought-iron balcony. 'Tis said he visits all the bedrooms in the dark of night, creaking up and down the staircase. Well, he must be very happy now that Phillip has filled the house with Roman, Egyptian and Etruscan sarcophagi. Adding to the Addams Family ambience of the hundred-year-old house, we've got bats in the bedrooms and bathrooms as well as the belfry.

I supervise the rewiring of thirteen rooms, six downstairs and five upstairs; a full inside paint job; the gutting and redesigning of the ugliest bathroom you could possibly imagine – brown shagpile carpet, mustard basins, a wardrobe alongside the shower recess. I come into constant contact with the past. Old newspapers in the attic, coins in the chimneys, the bones of dead dogs beneath the house. Restoration in this DIY age is meant to be satisfying, but to me it's a time-consuming, noisy, messy, expensive interruption.

The Wisemans started building our homestead in 1890, recording the fact with a sandstone plaque set in the red bricks made on the property. In a style common at the time from New England to South Yarra, it wasn't designed as a pretentious centrepiece for a feudal village, but as the hub of a big business. Nonetheless, it is a gracious building with fireplaces in every room, tall ceilings, French windows opening onto verandahs upstairs and down, north-facing bay windows, wrought iron for the balconies, and a classic galvanised-iron roof that you can see shining from the top of the mountain 10 kilometres away. The internal timber is Australian cedar. Under crusts of old paint and paper, the walls are in good condition. Along with the bathrooms, a jerry-built patio and a murky swimming pool were added in the 1960s. Otherwise the building, perched on its rocky knoll, is unspoiled. A house this size would once have had full-time maids (and later we unearth the ruins of their living quarters), but I'd never want such an intrusion on privacy. Though there are times when I'd welcome one of the cooks.

When reading articles about 'authentic' historical refurbishments of old, dark homesteads, I'm relieved that we're not doing it and therefore don't have to buy ghastly pieces of furniture simply because 'they are right for the period'. Nor do we have to hang bad paintings of long-dead relatives to prove our pedigree. In any case there wouldn't be any room, as Phillip has covered every inch of the walls with portraits of long-dead Egyptians. That's the only dynastic glory we celebrate.

The house has pull cords instead of light switches, and the electrician's apprentice has been asked to replace them while I spend the afternoon discussing cattle-yard design, a subject I don't begin to understand. 'The weaners will move better if we put the race this way,' says the man trying to sell us a set of prefab metal yards. These are the new fashion – quick, easy and supposedly cheaper to maintain than the old, charming, crafted wooden ones made of local timber and shaped with an axe.

I return home from this dirty, dusty, windy work to discover that the apprentice, working in ideal conditions, has got his job entirely wrong. Dangling from the 4-metre ceilings, the new brown pull cords are so short I have to stand on a chair to turn the lights on. In the dark, chair under my arm, I stumble from room to room fumbling for the unseen cords. The next morning I stand on the chair to demonstrate the problem. And the kid stares up in disbelief. He sheepishly raises his eyebrows, tries out a smile.

We were about to build a home for Reg and Yvonne when instead we purchased another 2000 hectares next door, complete with two more houses. In a few months, Elmswood has become 4000 hectares, comprising four houses, two shearing sheds, two hay sheds, stables, four river pumps along 6 kilometres of river. Why am I fussing with pull cords?

This new adjacent land, that so naturally extends our boundaries, gives the farm a more workable canvas and a greater opportunity to succeed as a business, but we'll need more help. JP, short for John Philip Gilbert, his wife Margaret and four children, Louise, Jenny, John and Matthew, have lived on the property for ten years. JP knows every ridge, tree, rocky knoll and river flat on the land. We ask the Gilberts to stay on.

The back country is wild, vertiginous, cool, and a place to get lost in, but nature provides signposts to help us find our way. A bent tree, Corot-style, provides a perfect arch to ride under. An evergreen gully often has echidnas waddling by. A giant rock resembles an elephant. There's a lot of land to learn. At times I think it's too much. A neighbour says that, after fifty years, he still doesn't know his place. 'You need more than a lifetime.' Years later we know this is true.

First the contour of the horizon imprints on my memory. It's the view from the homestead I see every day when feeding the chooks. To change the perspective, to understand this place better, I drive somewhere, anywhere, park and begin long, prickly, quiet walks. The only flat land is between the homestead and the river. Then come the curvaceous, lightly treed paddocks that Capability Brown would have approved of, then the property turns into high ridges and deep dramatic gullies leading towards the dark drama of the high hills. Only through these walks can I piece the geography together.

On weekends Phillip and I go further afield on our four-wheel bike. We give the thirty-seven paddocks names.

Some are simply descriptive: Dam, Blackflat, Hut, Kewell. Others, like Hospital, derive from anecdote or usage. I neatly write them on a huge aerial photograph. Though geography was my favourite subject at school, I always failed it. I don't want to fail this. I can't.

With a body battered by sixty years of hard work and harder drinking, Terry Quinn lives on a productive 2-hectare block next to ours. He grows vegetables, and his wife, the gentle, enduring Dulcie, grows gladioli. Phillip is enchanted by them because they so closely resemble the grandparents who raised him. Terry's worked here at Elmswood on and off for over forty-five years, as a shearer, a shepherd, a fencer. He fills us with his stories, and as he does they become our stories too.

Terry describes a time when Elmswood was marooned in prickly pear, impassably thick from the hills to the kitchen door, a bit like the Sleeping Beauty castle with nettles and thistles. He also remembers when the entire district was being destroyed by rabbits, and chuckles as he recalls how, instead of killing them all off as he was hired to do, he actually bred them, ensuring that superior bucks and does were saved from traps, ferrets and fumigation. 'Well, I wasn't going to put myself out of work!'

And there is the unforgettable day when he demonstrates

'whistling up foxes', calling vixens and their cubs from their hidden dens.

I ask Terry to help me, just a few hours a week. To plant trees, lift hay bales. He seems to say yes, but I'm not quite sure. He's had a heart attack. Has to be careful. 'I'll come Monday,' he muffles. To work? To talk more? Did I say something to offend him? Was $10 an hour an insult? I am uneasy with the laconic rural no-speak. On Monday he turns up with his hoe and instantly understands what needs doing. He knows our farm better than we do.

We decide to plant an avenue of trees from the bridge to the homestead, and I want to see white trunks. I photograph Terry at the side of the parched road to give me a 'before' photograph. A *Eucalyptus citriodora* I'd planted in the garden earlier has been killed by frost, so I start researching, seeking botanic information of white-trunked trees that might survive. As well, I read my Edna Walling and leaf through the photographs of Harold Cazneaux.

The driveway must look natural, even if the chosen species won't be native to the region. I plan a higgledy-piggledy planting and settle on *Eucalyptus scoparia*. It has white trunks and it's meant to be tough. But no sooner have we planted fifty than the Forestry Commission announces they're doomed. All the trees in the district have a bug and the commission has stopped selling them. I break the sad news to Phillip and tell him I'm going to pull them out immediately. Be done with it. But he fights for their lives.

'Leave them,' he says, 'be hopeful.' And now, fourteen years later, they arch proudly over the driveway that had been left barren and ugly for over a century.

I'd like to take an 'after' photograph with Terry but he's long since died. After years of helping me in so many ways, Terry departed with a mildly protesting Dulcie to the moonscape of Lightning Ridge, where he fossicked for opals until Dulcie died and he was diagnosed with cancer. In memory of him we've a 6-metre statue of Mercury that Phillip bought from a foundry in Florence; it stands just where Terry had stood for the 'before' photograph.

Because Elmswood wraps around one side of Gundy, it is inevitably part of the community. They're not houses I pass, but people's homes. I've their phone numbers on the Fire Brigade list that dangles behind the kitchen door. I've met just about everyone around here.

Yet every newcomer remains a threat. And people are cautious with me. They're not unfriendly, but perhaps my style of shooting my mouth off about anything and everything is inappropriate here. I find my lips sealing. There's a subtext I'm unclear about, until a couple of women arrive at the door eager to explain a few things.

The principal rule of our rural neighbourhood is to be polite at all times. Most people are invariably nice to your face. This is no bad thing as it keeps order. So even if you come from an argumentative world and regard a person as stupid, boring or corrupt, you still accept their dinner invitation. A neighbour puts it bluntly: 'Patrice, if you're not nice to everyone, they won't help you when you have a bushfire.'

There is nowhere to hide in the country. Anonymity is a myth. I am more exposed here than when I was part of the television publicity machine. Then, I was simply portrayed as one of the many clichéd personalities, someone, 'happy' to join the news team, 'thrilled' to be on television, 'successful' and earning loads of money to boot.

We are pears in an apple basket here. To the local aristocracy, we're nouveau riche. Our city earnings have made Elmswood ours, but for them new money isn't real money. It's better to have had money than to have it now. Others, too, are resentful, assuming Elmswood to be a large hobby farm, not a business investment. 'You won't need to make money from your farm,' says a local. Of course not, I always throw money away!

It's hard to grasp why so many farms around us are going broke. As we arrive, cattle prices are enjoying a temporary boom and wool has never been better. Yet the land isn't sustaining them any more, and farmer after farmer is applying to the council for subdivision approval. As land is traded, a new social order is formed.

One of the great Australian delusions is that we live in a

classless society. It's nonsense in the city and bullshit in the bush. Wool producers were like Britain's landed gentry, used to having the most clout in rural society. But their fleeces drifted away like clouds. Next it was beef that ruled the roost, but its tenure too has grown shaky. Nowadays other rural enterprises earn considerably more income, and the beef producer shares the top rung of the social ladder with vignerons, horse breeders, niche food growers, and the increasingly powerful cotton farmers. Sam Shepard's memorable line, 'If you ain't a cowboy you ain't shit,' certainly doesn't ring true around here.

One cattle breeder, soon to leave the district, tells me, 'Quantity of land disguises bad management. Mistakes spread over a thousand hectares can be hard to see.' Land has always been bought and sold, but today the motivations are very different to those of even twenty years ago. Now the productive value of the land is rarely a consideration for the purchaser. Land is desired for its landscape value, its beauty, its semi-isolation. (A good small block surrounded by farmland sells at a premium.) Now, alongside people who make a living from the land are people who don't, and deep conflicts arise.

Nonetheless, there's still a lot of cow counting going on. It amuses me when people ask, 'How big is your breeding herd?' I watch their faces as they make a quick calculation, multiplying the cows by, say, $500 each, then puzzle why you've invested millions in such an unprofitable enterprise.

Of course I'm adding up the numbers as well. Again and again, trying to convince myself we're going to be all right financially. With so much land, how can we not make a living? It's a case of what we expect, of how much is enough. Farming won't make us richer, that's for sure. That we accept. Had money been our sole motive, we'd have gone into real estate or the share market.

According to modern economic theory, to make the most of things, we have to produce what the market wants. Otherwise we'll become just another farm producing what no one wants to buy. Yet our first question is not 'What does the market want?' but rather 'What can the land here produce?' With a century's infrastructure for beef and wool in place, we decide to maintain that tradition for a few more years. Just before the wool prices collapse, we sell the flocks to focus on beef, but all the time we're thinking about what else is possible, and appropriate. Dozens of crops are rejected because they're too thirsty or pose other environmental risks. But what about walnut trees for nuts and veneer? Or grapes? Or herbs? Or alpacas? Or emus? What about kangaroo meat? The list gets long, the files thicken.

We finally settle on planting an olive grove.

We lean against our wooden cattle yards while buyers move amongst the big and bad-mannered cattle, giving them the once-over. We're selling our rogues, the brutes that uproot fences and smash the antique railings, splintering the shiny, rubbed wood I'm so fond of. A buyer for a supermarket takes one pen, a cattle dealer another.

I'm learning what a good cow, steer and bull should be according to the latest research and fashion, and conclude that lean beef is what we need to produce. This is the message from meat research institutes and market surveys, circa 1987. But a decade later, lean beef is passé and marbled meat – fat within the muscle – is in. No sooner do I understand all the various specifications than they change. During thirteen years of trading, we'll sell big, small, fat and lean cattle with infused European and *Bos indicus* blood lines. The market is always right, but it's always changing its mind.

British breeds are fat breeds. Our idea is that if we cross them with *indicus* breeds, like the marvellous Brahman, not only will we get hybrid vigour, always an outcome of cross-breeding, but also lean, state-of-the-art beef. A few farmers around the district are already experimenting with their herds. All the research aside, we like the look of cows with floppy ears and humps. Brahmans, the cows of India. How exciting!

Soon, Phillip and I are searching the steep hills of coastal New South Wales for Brahman bulls. We pull up at one place and see a pen brimming with them. Phillip, known in media circles as 'the man in black' and appropriately dressed on this occasion, spots a black Brahman amongst the mob. It is love at first sight. Phillip climbs the railings, pushes aside the brown and white ones before making his way to the black giant, which promptly puts its huge head on his shoulder and gazes dreamily into his eyes.

Back home in the paddock he looks majestic. Phillip names him Malcolm, after Malcolm X, and he dominates our bull herd for years, not because he is especially virile but because he has influence with the boss. Phillip would call him like a dog and Malcolm would come trotting over a 200-hectare paddock and lift him off the ground with his head. But Malcolm became rather cocky in his old age, and a regular roaming pain-in-the-ass, pulling down fences, trailing wire and posts like a necklace, until one day, when JP and I were loading cows for the export abattoir, we quickly ran Malcolm up the cattle race and onto the truck. Phillip's never quite forgiven me.

After six years of developing a herd of Brahman-cross cows, we found ourselves in the middle of a drought, hand-feeding a lot of big animals. Now we're sticking to the original Hereford and Angus lines, and all the cross-breeding has stopped. And when people ask what sort of meat we produce and expect an answer like, 'Two hundred kilograms over-the-hook, zero dentition, averaging 10 millilitres fat with a B muscle score,' I say provocatively, 'Well, tasty, tender and certified biodynamic beef. This is a farm, not a factory.'

I can no longer avoid the reality of the abattoir. It's time for a blooding. Many city people can't face what really happens on farms. Whether it's sheds full of chooks or pigs or cattle and sheep, the fact is we breed them to kill. For city people to eat.

Early on I'd introduced myself to the local abattoir manager and asked for a tour of the works. He gave me a cool appraisal before making the enigmatic observation, 'You're either in the beef business or the beauty business.'

We walk to the pens where the animals are hosed down before being shot in the head with a mushroom gun. We wash our hands, put on paper caps and white coats, and enter the main killing floor. I stand amongst the hanging carcasses and hear wolf whistles – I am somewhat flattered until I learn they've mistaken me for the new meat inspector and are whistling to alert each other.

As I walk past the bodies swinging on their hooks, I feel entirely unshocked. Only recently have I realised that, although I've been to the abattoir a hundred times, I've never really watched the process. Today will be different. I'll force myself to *really look* at what happens to the animals we produce, and not focus only on abstracts like the computer printout attached to the carcass once it's lined up in the cool room.

So I do *really look* when Mick puts the gun to a steer's head and kills it. And *really look* when Peter puts the hook behind the tendon near the hoof to hang it up. And *really look* when Brett cuts off the head and skins the face. And *really look* when Roy inspects it and cuts out the cheek and tongue. And *really look* when John saws the decapitated carcass in half. And *really look* when Paul trims off the fat and Tony dumps the guts down the chute. And *really look* as Simon hoses away the blood. And I *really learn* that the whole thing is shockingly shocking.

Yet I still want to produce meat and eat it.

John Embling, who runs the Families in Distress Foundation in Melbourne, dealing with disturbed children, tells me that slaughtermen frequently have dysfunctional lives. Institutionalised killing must have its effect.

Learning about breeding beef is only half the equation, selling it the other. In the past, producers rarely knew for whom they were producing their meat. Truckloads were simply taken to the sale yards and, depending on who was bidding that day, could end up anywhere. While sale yards are cultural icons that most shires would hate to see go, the savvy producers today sell directly to shops, organise brands or sign production contracts with meat wholesalers. I suspect I'll live to see the end of the sale-yard system.

To help understand the marketing end of the equation I begin to cook and eat a lot of beef. What can I do with all this topside? Should I chuck out chuck steak?

In 1987 Scone had four butcher shops, but it was the enthusiasm of two brothers, Michael and Murray at Towler Family Butchery, who impressed me. They used to run a regular sort of shop until one day they took their pie machine to work and made a couple of beef pies for lunch out of left-over mince. People commented on the delicious smells wafting from the back room. Days later they were offering pies to their customers. Word spread quickly that the butcher shop's pies were made with real beef! Suddenly, they quadrupled their customer base. Soon they were making quiche, lasagne, casseroles, and cooking roast dinners. A new kitchen had to be built, a full-time cook hired. Meat industry awards were won and plaques showed off on the counter. It was in the back rooms of Towler's that I really began to learn about beef.

I'd asked Michael and Murray to butcher some meat for us after restaurants expressed interest in biodynamic beef. None wanted to buy the whole beast, only certain portions. On the first day, I took in my new official butchering manuals, with beautiful photography and correct nomenclature. I wanted each portion of meat to look exactly like the photograph. As we started to break up the body – that is, bone out the carcass – I found myself surrounded by blobs of meat I couldn't identify. Some cuts were obvious but others just looked like bloodied muscle. Even now, after years of doing it, there's usually a moment or two of total confusion. Butchering is a highly skilled trade.

Soon we were doing home deliveries. Although there weren't many, this brought us directly in touch with customers who bought our 15 kilograms of mixed cuts in a package. It was fascinating to learn first-hand what people were cooking and why they preferred certain cuts. We experimented with sausages, including one made with lean mince beef, salt, pepper, chives and no preservatives.

In Ruth L. Ozeki's book *My Year of Meat* (Picador, 1998) a desperate, out-of-work documentary filmmaker takes on a project to promote US meat in Japan. A memo lands across her desk explaining that meat consumption is now a signifier of status in Japan and pointing out that 'Pork and other meats is [sic] second class meats, so please remember this easy motto: Pork is Possible but Beef is Best.'

Why didn't I think of that when we started selling Elmswood Beef?

'Luv, mistakes happen,' said the owner of the abattoir when I demanded a guarantee that my meat wouldn't get mixed up. Not surprisingly, his abattoir went broke. Today, the new owners are keen to provide quality assurances as they improve their facilities in preparation for globalisation. In this case, global pressures have helped lift standards.

In the first year I learn everything I can about the land. In the second year about plants. In the third about animals.

In the fourth I try to piece it all together. When we decide to become biodynamic, our decision confirms the worst suspicions of the neighbours. Not only are we communists (I beg Phillip to stop mentioning he was a member of the Communist Party!), but we're also stark raving mad. A farm without sprays? Without drenches? Without superphosphate? We'll be destroyed by weeds, by insects, by disease.

I dislike the expression 'chemical-free food'. It's entirely inaccurate, given that we are, after all, made of chemicals. It's a question of which chemicals are involved. Why shouldn't food be as unadulterated as possible? As clean as possible? So we use no manufactured chemicals in production. It's not as if we live in hope that nothing will go wrong, we're always on the lookout, prepared for disasters, thinking about tactics, experimenting with alternatives to the dreaded tin drum.

We're not simply organic farmers, we're biodynamic, an oddly high-tech term for a traditional approach. While biodynamic producers are *always* organic – that is, we never use artificial fertilisers or pesticides – the reverse is not the case. The biodynamic system, explained in more detail later, involves much more than simply not using industrial chemicals. And yet it's not just what we don't do that makes biodynamics so special – it's very proactive. The ultimate in mixed farming. A way of thinking. A little like eating: if you have a sense of the food that makes you feel well, you can often avoid being unwell. You can organise your eating habits to maintain good health. So too with farming.

Biodynamics shouldn't be about producing food for the rich, to be sold at a premium. It's the way things should be done, or at least, to use current jargon, it should be 'a stretch goal', for *all* agricultural industries.

Some farmers try – no, half try – an organic or biodynamic approach and find it all gets too much. Weeds drive them to despair, thistles wave over their heads and they surrender to the quick chemical fix. Successful certified biodynamic farmers say no to the use of chemicals. Full stop. End of story. We replace an addiction to chemicals with long-term commitment. As these days commitment to anything is often regarded as foolish and old-fashioned, we march to the beat of a different drum. The temptation of the quick fix just isn't there. We hear a deeper rhythm and accept all that it entails. Our core belief is that healthy farming begins with healthy soil.

Biodynamics offers no easy answers to problems. In the beginning I wanted fellow biodynamic farmers to tell me what to do, but they wouldn't. Each of us has had to adjust biodynamics to suit our particular circumstances and intentions. I had to learn to work within a framework, to make my own decisions. One of the hardest things early on was that, despite meeting many successful biodynamic farmers, I felt I was isolated. Every farmer is, in a way, just as every patch of earth is different: in moisture level, drainage, structure, trace elements. When a consultant rattles off facts like one would the five-times table, I'm immediately suspicious. Clearly humans have an innate desire to reduce everything, including biodynamic agriculture, to rigid rules and regulations, but it can't be done.

Some biodynamic farmers feel like old favourite books. They are wise, insightful people and you can read their properties and look at the illustrations. You can see they're doing the right thing. Despite constant obstacles, these farmers have learned to maintain an equanimity. None of them are rich but they regard themselves as blessed and lucky.

Industrial chemical agriculture is like bad television. There's too much of it around and it's impossible to avoid. Every rural newspaper is packed with stories about the latest chemical attack for this or that pest, or a new artificial fertiliser to boost crops. We have to overlook advertorials, stop reading the junk sent out with the bills: 'Buy this drench and get a free drum of poison.'

One third of Australia's cultivation land is already affected by salinity, yet we still massacre trees at the same rate as Brazil. And the crops we choose to grow and the areas we use as cattle runs compound the problem. Everyone, even the National Farmers Federation, agrees on one thing: agriculture needs a fundamental shift in attitude if we're to survive. Current practices are unsustainable. And an exaggeration to say that biodynamics can bring dead soils back to life.

When I return from a quick visit to Adelaide, the pile of mail on the kitchen table is toppling over. After making a cup of green tea, the deep pleasure of opening letters – as opposed to bills – begins. Over the years I've felt pangs of envy at the massive volume of interesting correspondence Phillip receives. So when there's more for me I am, to say the least, chuffed. It is a varied selection this day, some with impressive overseas stamps. A couple of long personal letters, garden journals, seed catalogues, a newsletter about worms in sheep, a book on honey and pollen flora, and a long envelope with my name written in backhand. I suspect it is a camouflaged advertisement and scoop it up with the rubbish to dump in the bin. On an impulse I open it and an invitation to an information day about olives falls out. Hmmm. I phone my acceptance immediately. 'I just sent a few out to those I thought might be interested,' says Helen Sinclair, manager of the Scone Business Centre.

A few weeks later, on a glorious October spring day, I head off to the Scone Research Service Centre on Gundy Road for the meeting. More than a hundred locals arrive at the same time. Squeezed next to me in the crowded room is a beef producer who immediately announces he hates olive oil and only uses it for keeping his saddle in good nick. His son, sitting on his other side, confesses he's never tried it but thinks it sounds pretty yucky. The room is full of people like this father and son who certainly aren't there for any love of olives. They have no tales to tell about sitting under an olive tree in the Greek Isles reciting Byron, or roaming the hills of Tuscany. 'It's peasant work,' I overhear a fine-wool producer say. 'In Europe, all you ever see are women in black and old men working the groves.'

I like seeing peasants in groves, I think, with their World War II parachutes spread out underneath gnarled silvery trees to catch falling olives. What's wrong with peasants? A woman weaves through the crowds at lunchtime and asks earnestly, 'Have you ever heard of a rich olive grower, Patrice?' Come to think of it, I haven't. But so what? There are thousands of growers and millions of olive trees, what do I know?

Most people have come today because they are searching desperately for any farm venture that can give them an income. All day we look at spreadsheets, watch films, hear stories, and dip white bread in bowls of oil, while in the back of our minds we wonder if olives can ever be a real, dinky-di, financially viable industry.

Throughout the day, whenever someone says anything vaguely useful I record it. My notes, scribbled across the handouts, are to be the start of my olive education. I can't pronounce the varieties of olives: Fran-toy-oh (Frantoio),

Le-chee-no (Leccino), Man-za-nil-la. Repeating these poetic sounds over and over, I remember Nabokov playing with the sexual sound of the name Lolita: Lo-lee-tah. How the lips move. My misspelt list of varieties includes two we'll ultimately plant, the frost-hardy Californian Mission, not so beautiful to say, and the celebrated Tuscan variety Correggiola. Or, to be more accurate, rolling my tongue to give that authentic Italian 'r' sound, Cor-reg-gee-oh-lah!

We wave goodbye, knowing that something, we're not quite sure what, is about to happen. There's a feeling in the air. Optimism. Excitement. Over the next few weeks we rehearse the names of varieties, begin to digest some facts, and meet again, this time at a vineyard where long ago the Italian owners planted a small olive grove.

This gathering is more serious. We begin the day with a brief show-and-tell, announcing our names and saying why we've come. There are representatives from the landed gentry who boast about their dynastic properties. A young tycoon from Sydney brags about the sale of his franchise business and his hundreds of millions to invest. I mumble that my name is Patrice Newell from Gundy and I have a biodynamic property, at which point I lose all confidence.

At lunch I have an argument with an agricultural bureaucrat who insists that farmers like me are ratbags and that I'll never be able to keep an olive grove biodynamic. And he goes onto defame another biodynamic farmer. I am ropeable and let him know it. On arriving home, fury unsubsided, I phone the New South Wales Department of Agriculture and threaten a formal complaint, only to be told that my antagonist is taking a redundancy and becoming, alas, a consultant.

Once people just talked, now they consult. Consultants are a product of our times. Farm consultants are principally people who've been pushed out of the once extensive Department of Agriculture network throughout the state; they've been privatised. In the mid-eighties almost every small town had advisers for whatever industries were in the area. Scone had a dairy officer, livestock adviser, agronomist, and a fully operational office where anyone could receive information. Theirs were essential services. But with economic irrationalism marching on, thousands – often the best people – took redundancies. Scone lost an agronomist, who, yes, became a consultant. Eighteen months later, the department, realising their mistake, had to hire another one.

In 1989, with much hoopla, the New South Wales Department of Agriculture hired Michael Burlace, a former livestock officer with the department, as its first full-time organic officer. Michael advised farms of all types, collected loads of information, and eventually wrote an Australian manual for organic farmers and students. At that stage the organic/biodynamic food industry in Australia was valued at $100 million. In 1996 Michael became a full-time father and took a redundancy – it was months before he was replaced.

Soon after we arrived at Elmswood a friend of Phillip's phoned to rave about a professor of agriculture who'd recently designed a management plan for his farm. For $500 dollars the professor would move in for a weekend, roam about your farm and tell you what you should do. After such a strong endorsement we invited him to visit. He arrived late one Friday night, expecting a three-course meal and conversation. After breakfast on Saturday I asked, 'Well, what's the program now?'

'You make a basket of sandwiches, Patrice,' he commanded, 'then we'll have a drive.'

This was during the empty pantry days, so making a basket of sandwiches was no easy feat. I managed something but was so put out by the request it probably tasted like fresh snail. We spent the day driving around and every time I asked a direct question like 'What's the name of that grass?' or 'Does this soil colour indicate low iron?' or 'Why do the cattle lick that rock?' he had no answers. He was more interested in gossiping about the local gentry. A few weeks later his written report and bill arrived. We were shocked by the vacuity of the former given the size of the latter. A high-school student could have done a better job.

Now I have a clear expectation of consultants when hiring them. Firstly, they must know more than I do. Secondly, they must be articulate. Imagine, for example, hiring an art critic to teach you about *Whistler's Mother*. It wouldn't be good enough if they said, 'Well, it's a nice picture of an old lady sitting on a chair in profile.' I want to be helped to see and understand, whether it's about *Whistler's Mother* or an olive grove. Unfortunately, too many farm advisers have no practical experience. The best advisers are farmers.

Once we've settled on the romantic idea of planting our own grove, we're faced with the practical decision of where to put it. Choosing the site should be a high point in our adventure, but anxiety almost spoils things before they begin. Contemplating the permanence of olive trees, I realise I am used to seeing movement in the paddocks. Cattle constantly change the landscape, clustering under trees in the heat of the day, and spreading out across the hills at dusk like fish moving in water. And I can reposition them whenever I like.

Our latest fantasies have us strolling at sunset amongst shimmering olive leaves, wild flowers at our feet. Or at harvest time, sweat scarves tied around our foreheads, stacking the wine cellar with stainless-steel vats of oil. I imagine giving a bottle of Elmswood oil and a jar of Elmswood honey to every visitor. I'll become a more generous person when we have an olive grove.

For ten years we've been learning about the nooks and crannies of Elmswood, extending the boundaries, adding our own secrets to its history. We've been pushing outwards ever since we arrived. Now the time has come to bring the focus back home. I have to make this decision at a time when Rory is starting school, when the pace of the day will be dictated by school bus timetables and homework. Starting farm work at dawn isn't going to be so easy for the next few years, and you can't do everything during school holidays, so I want the grove to be as conveniently positioned as possible.

At first I set my heart on Timmy's Paddock, named in honour of our first, beloved cattle dog, run over by a neighbour. It's a 20-hectare treeless rectangle visible from my kitchen-sink window, half a kilometre away as the crow flies but a bumpy one kilometre by four-wheel drive. This south-facing window frames one of the great views from the house. Phillip has positioned his sixteenth-century French terracotta fountain with its cluster of cherubs and dolphins just outside the window, and I've planted box, honeysuckle, and tall, bearded yellow iris around it. I can always hear water and watch the birds bathing while I'm cooking. Beyond this is a cornucopia of double wisteria, and then the ground slopes down to the river before rising once more to Timmy's. To glimpse the olive grove in the distance would be an even better way to start the day. There I'd be, standing in the kitchen, rinsing out the porridge bowls, and the olive grove would beckon.

We test the soil and find it's near perfect, well drained and gravelly with all the right minerals, an alkaline pH. We've deep-ripped the hillside for lucerne and pasture, and the soil structure is now aerated. It's ready to have olives planted in neat rows across the slope.

The top end of Timmy's is near the bitumen road that takes tourists up and over the dramatic Barrington Tops National Park. There our grove would stand, telling the world that we were in the olive business, not only the beef business. I'd put up a sign: BIODYNAMIC OLIVES PLANTED 1996. But having the grove at the edge of the property would mean we'd have less control. I consider putting an additional fence inside Timmy's, leaving a lane between the two as extra insurance against roaming cattle or sheep. We've never done an accurate measurement but the boundaries of Elmswood must run at least 60 kilometres and we have a total of fifteen other properties bordering ours. Sharing the work of keeping fences erect, trying to ensure each others' animals remain in their respective places isn't simple. And although there's no immediate cause for concern, land does get sold and a new owner might plant some chemical-dependent crop next to our biodynamic olive grove.

Add water to my concerns, and things aren't looking

good for Timmy's. Getting water from the river up to the top of the paddock would be no easy task. A pipe would have to dangle high across the river, yet even a moderate flood would snag it, dragging it down as uprooted trees rose and sank in the brown raging water. We'd have to put up another tank, which would be very conspicuous from just about everywhere, especially my kitchen window.

There is another issue: our olive trees could be alive centuries after we're forgotten and the house has fallen down, and if this is to be a successful venture then a capacity to grow as a business is essential. Timmy's could only accommodate five thousand trees.

Finally, it is the possibility of personal embarrassment that rules Timmy's out. The prospect of working so close to passing traffic is intolerable. Everyone would see me – not only the sign – especially when I was planting, bent over, on my knees, bum in the air. Would people toot? Would I be offended if they didn't? And if our venture failed it would look awful, an exposed mistake.

Other options for the grove would impinge on our cattle operations. We need this paddock for hay, this one for silage, this one for access to the cattle yards, and while I believe olives will be more profitable in the long term, we can't jeopardise the beef business.

And olives might not be happy at Elmswood, a possibility I try not to think about. My good friend Lyn bought a picturesque farm outside Maleny, in Queensland. Down from her house, in a wind-free pocket, are the sad remains of a failed kiwifruit orchard. The previous owner had obviously spent a lot of money on trellising and irrigation and the orchard could be resurrected, but we know it will never happen. Why had it gone wrong? Was it a question of scale? Too small to be viable? We hear that nine out of ten businesses fail in the city. They fail in the country too. I don't want to fail, at least not publicly.

Back home I spread maps and aerial photos of the property across the kitchen table. Staring at these doesn't provide the inspiration I'm looking for but triggers an important thought. If we are to grow into a big olive operation we should spread the risk. We should have more than one grove, experimenting with different parts of the property. I'll have no monoculture here. Each new grove will be an ecosystem in itself.

Roaming like some demented creature, I range across bare hills, ever further away.

'You'll work out the right place, Patrice,' says Phillip, weary of the endless discussions on site selection. Normally I find his trust in my abilities soothing. He's a modern man, able to step aside and let me get on with the business of the farm. But this time I resent the responsibility of having to make the decision alone. I feel like Michael Collins being sent over to London by DeValera to negotiate Irish independence, knowing I'm about to get into deep shit.

Phillip keeps reminding me of one of the few management principles he found effective: 'It's better to make a wrong decision than no decision at all, Patrice.' Not in this case. He positions an ancient Roman senator of solid marble amongst the peach blossom, a row of Balinese temple gods along a pathway between the figs and plums. Why aren't I being so decisive?

I meet people who are buying land specifically for olive groves. Oh for a nice neat little 40-hectare block! They aren't facing the anxieties 4000 hectares can produce.

Weeks are passing and I am still avoiding a final decision. Then, late one afternoon, driving back relaxed and alert with Phillip and Rory after a day spent at the back of the furthest paddock, where we'd walked along gullies, checked fences, cooked sausages over wood coals, scooped creek water into cupped hands, I realise something. One of the difficulties in trying to visualise our paddocks differently has been the imposition, over the last hundred years, of fence lines. I was being fenced in by old fences. Most have been erected gridlike, without consideration to natural contours. As we drive down from the airstrip there's a great vista of the homestead and surrounding area, a view of vastness and domestic intimacy in one frame. As I open a gate, shooing fat cows away, I see it. What I've been trying to see. An olive grove, in my mind. There, right before me. I mentally erase the fences, the cattle, and move the neurotic alpaca and our pet sheep – the head-butting

Lametta. And there they are, our first two thousand olive trees around the shearing shed.

Back at the homestead, I run to the kitchen, grab the Nikon and race back to the shed where, as the sky transforms into a clean, lemony twilight, I take pictures of the pasture now designated for olives. Until now it's been called Horse Paddock, the place where on so many days I've lifted Rory up onto her pony to walk them up and down the soft hills above the Pages River. It was here that she grew to love horses, had her first trot and canter, fell off, got back on. I've walked every inch of the paddock, awaiting the annual burst of wild zinnias under the yellow box, picking rocks for the garden, chipping burrs, and sitting, feet dangling over the cliff, plopping stones into our favourite stretch of the river.

I walk past the shed and the two-seater galvo loo, once used by shearers, and a hundred-year-old slab hut, originally the shearers' kitchen, now full of boxes recording forty years of Phillip's life. Sometimes we go down to sort through the chaos, laughing over letters and finding photos of Phillip when he had hair. Now the boxes, stacked to the roof, are to be collected by the National Library. But we might change our minds. Phillip's life – the forty-seven years before me – has been stored in that hut for years. I think I'll miss it if it goes.

Snap, snap. The light fades. I've taken a roll of film.

There'll be no Silent Spring here.

In his 1998 Boyer Lectures *A Spirit of Play: The Making of Australian Consciousness* (ABC Books, 1998), David Malouf complained of Australian environmentalists using 'evangelical and apocalyptic language' and having a 'hectoring self-righteousness'. He's right. There is a sour theme running through factions of the ecological movement, but to many the language of Armageddon seems the only way to attract attention. When I see young men and women on the news chaining themselves to trees and bulldozers, waving banners, shouting and weeping their concerns, I feel proud. 'Goodonya,' I'll say to the TV, guilty of sitting in comfort while they passionately and physically commit themselves to the cause. If their arguments were poetically expressed, would that make them more true?

The United States, a nation with endless environmental disasters, had Thoreau, Emerson and Rachel Carson to help latter-day ecologists find context and understanding. In Australia that burden has been the responsibility of nature poets and landscape painters, rather than writers. For me, no Australian author has been the equivalent of Thoreau, who celebrated nature as he described and questioned it. 'Nature' isn't a word we use much in Australia. I wish we did. 'The bush', beloved of Lawson but used around here as a pejorative, doesn't have the same ring to it. The bush for many is merely an immense wasteland undeserving of concern. In the absence of the romance created by a Thoreau, landscape can be destroyed without arousing any heartfelt response.

I remember Phillip and I laughing during the first national conference on the greenhouse effect, set up by his Commission for the Future in 1986. The conference gathered people into halls across Australia, connecting them via satellite and giant television screens, where the faithful heard stories about melting icecaps, seas rising by 2 metres. Many were palpably disappointed when a visiting scientist produced computer modelling suggesting the sea would rise by as little as 2 centimetres. They wanted the full catastrophe, a last judgement to punish us for the excesses of capitalism and human greed. And the same group was outraged by the revelation that many of the dangerous emissions weren't coming from factory chimneys or car exhausts, but from termite mounds, rice paddies and the flatulence of ruminants.

City people are the most passionately apocalyptic, reading books with titles like *Dying Forests, Green or Gone, Continent in Crisis, Our Stolen Future*, whereas most farmers are too busy or too tired to read much beyond farm catalogues and the weekly rural newspapers, in which environmental matters are either downplayed, shamelessly ignored or treated with contempt. Except when governments try to implement laws on salinity, native pasture or water pollution, and then there's outrage. I belong to what feels like a small group at the coalface, trying to negotiate between the apocalyptists and those unwilling to see.

Hardly a day passes where I don't ask myself what the hell is going on. The farm is my laboratory, biodynamics my experiment. This is where I try to make sense of the world. I know I'll find answers, as long as I keep focused. What would I feel if we didn't have a farm? Distress or relief? Would the destruction of forests, soil salinisation, acidity, desertification and polluted rivers bother me half as much as losing the car keys? Would I place the environment in a niche along with the republic and reconciliation and perhaps make some tax-deductible donations?

Coming here I did what I naturally do in any new place, seek comfort and knowledge in books. There was so much to learn. First, history books. Who were the Wonnarua tribe? Where did they live? Which white men came to the Hunter Valley first? Who was Hunter? Who was first in the race to grab fertile land? What did the women do? What vegetables were grown? Who designed the interesting homesteads and shearing sheds? Then came the books of criticism and alarm, all sharing the central thesis that the natural world was being ruined. I was confronted by Bill McKibben's book *The End of Nature* (Random House, 1989), where he argues that we've already destroyed it. Just as people need to believe there's a God out there, they like to think that Nature is out there too, enduring and invincible. He ridicules the idea that Nature 'will change gradually and imperceptibly, if at all'. If we believe such nonsense, it's 'the result of a subtly warped perspective'.

A subtly warped perspective. Do I have that?

Reading makes me more and more depressed. I know too much about the problems, but too little for solutions. Theories aren't helping, yet it sometimes seems you can't do anything without them. I'm a product of an age when there's a theory for everything. No wonder we're all confused. But I know – and this is not a theory – that theories come and go, and most have the shelf-life of yoghurt. Even the intuition that tells you something is right or wrong evaporates. Yet the truth you feel is probably right.

There are none so blind as those who will not see. Our river is dwindling away. For much of the year the foot valve on the pump is choked with algae. But still some farmers on the river say, 'No worries.'

I lose my temper. 'Look at it. It's changing. Changing for the worse. It's obvious. It's self-evident.' But the evidence before their eyes isn't enough. They demand scientific proof, even though science is dynamic, its truths forever changing. In the meantime we have to make decisions based on our own observations.

We live in what social philosopher Anthony Giddens, in *Conversations with Anthony Giddens: Making Sense of Modernity* (Polity Press, 1998), calls a 'risk society, where history offers no guarantees'. The impact of the risks and decisions we're taking today will be hard to gauge in the future because the effects will be so diffuse. In a world where we can't have everything, it's possible, even likely, that what we're doing to the planet will be irreparable. According to Giddens, affluence is producing problems which can't be dealt with by more affluence. We certainly have a 'post-scarcity economy' – the scarce goods are clean air, good water, and food without toxic residue. So here I am, at little Gundy, trying to find a balance, a path, a sustainable way of farming amidst what Giddens calls 'information smog'.

In *Why Men Don't Iron* (HarperCollins 1998) Anne and Bill Moir use organic farming to dramatise the differences between men and women. They ridicule the whole organic approach, insisting that it demands more work and greater costs, that it halves the yields while doubling the amount of land required. The organic movement, to them, is a hobby horse for hobby farmers who can afford to waste money, time and effort. Moreover, they claim, it results in a poorer product.

The Moirs believe that all the touchy-feely sentiments about looking after the land come from eco-feminists getting the upper hand. They insist that most people studying organic courses and joining environmental groups in England, at least, are female, and that they're undermining man's dominance over nature. How exciting! And all this time I thought the organic/biodynamic movement was injecting commonsense into the debate. Now I learn I'm part of a feminist conspiracy whose 'alternative science' is part of the general dumbing down of the world. According to the Moirs, men confront 'a tough competitive wilderness' while women find 'a holistic garden of innocence'. So when the next developer wants to drain a wetland (do women ever want to drain wetlands?), or the local piggery dumps effluent into the watercourse, I must realise that it's all just part of nature.

When traditional farmers ask me suspiciously, aggressively, 'Well, how does biodynamics work?' I ask them, 'How does your system work?' All farmers – traditional, biodynamic, organic – work around the edges of many sciences: botany, biology, agronomy, chemistry. But farming is like cooking, more art than science, full of hope and guesswork.

There's so much food grown in the world today that it upsets the balance of production and triggers rows about trade, social structures and subsidies. Yet science is relentlessly pushing the frontiers of production, growing unlikely crops in unlikely places, and decisions by agricorps can cause cultural, political and economic upheaval across the globe, from rural villages in India to Gundy.

And now, thanks to science and the ludicrous arguments about us not being able to feed ourselves in the future (it's not a supply problem, but a price–distribution problem), we have genetic engineering (GE), which is *not* a continuation of the natural evolution of plant development, and *not* the same as hybridisation. It's too early to be categorical that this development will not have a negative effect on human health, despite the soothing statements issued by everyone from Monsanto to the CSIRO. No one can know.

With the exception of consumers in the United States, the rest of the world has greeted GE food with trepidation. Every Australian survey states that up to 80% of consumers are worried. The conservative rural newspaper *The Land* reacted with a cover story (15 April 1999) headed 'Gene Food Farce' and called for 'a major government-backed public education program'. This faithfully echoed the line pushed by the chemical companies selling GE seed stock. How can companies expecting to profit from these foods have the cheek to ask governments to pay for their advertising campaign?

A 1999 survey conducted by the food industry emphasised that consumers wanted 'integrity' in food. While the cynics dismiss this as being nostalgic, others, like Phillip and me, see no harm in giving people a choice between high-tech and old-fashioned food. The worry is that the environmental impact of GE food will render it eventually impossible to grow biodynamic food because GE seed and pollen will have proliferated everywhere, thus making GE food compulsory, with a half-dozen companies dominating the world's food supply. Just as another half-dozen dominate the world's media.

When we bought Elmswood we read about the possibility of food joining the technological superhighway. Now it has. And we're more certain than ever that we don't want to be part of it.

Trendy in New Age circles for years, the concept of 'holistic' has now entered the paddock, and the vocabulary of agriculture. Environmentalists are right when they argue for a holistic approach to a problem, but can the truth, the whole truth of a situation ever be calculated and measured? A fellow biodynamic producer faxes me a cartoon which shows a farmer standing alongside his giant biodynamic carrot. A scientist looking at the carrot says, 'But we need proof.'

When I read stories in the rural press about how this or that chemical has been successful in 'controlling' (never eradicating) a certain weed or insect, there is no mention of Anthony Giddens' risk factors, the pollution caused by the alleged cure – whether there's a long-term effect on the soil, how birds are affected when they innocently munch a poisoned seed – let alone by the entire manufacturing process of the chemical. Such problems are holistic by nature and therefore demand a holistic response.

Farmers impose their hopes on the land. To fence is to reshape. To plough is to patchwork, giving new colour and texture to the environment. But these hopes have a productive purpose. What could be more marvellous than to make food, fibre, timber? Is there to be less joy or celebration in a harvest? Am I like a child trying to put the square block in a round hole?

We now know the damage that hard-hoofed animals

have done to Australia, and I know I'm contributing to global warming because my cattle release so much methane. I know too that growing beef requires more water than growing wheat. I know that no matter how careful we are we cannot help but hurt the land. What I'm striving to do is make as little damage as possible.

We'd been at Elmswood only days when a local representative of the New South Wales Farmers Association came knocking, seeking my membership. I invited him in, accepted the brochures and offered tea. And as I poured, I kept laughing to myself, knowing that if this man knew me he wouldn't be asking for my endorsement.

Finally I had to admit to it. 'Sorry, but I could never be a member of the Farmers Association.' He looked at me, not understanding what I meant. 'It's too hard to explain,' I concluded, realising there were too many reasons for my animosity. Since the amicable Rick Farley left the National Farmers Federation the farmers' lobby groups have been on the wrong side of every issue: Mabo, Wik, national parks, chemicals, genetic engineering, subdivision, water usage, tree clearing.

But while turning away from conservative rural clubs, I joined other groups. I needed to find kindred spirits as we set about turning our property into a business. I've got to know a lot of good people who are trying to make a decent, honest living from their land, and those who are succeeding are families with strong philosophical beliefs. They put a lot of thought into every decision. They take the time to step back and consider things. They have been the best of teachers.

For some families the routine of the day, the week, the months has changed little over a century. On Saturday afternoons they play sport with their neighbours. They never work on Sundays; some go to church, others simply take time to reflect and replenish themselves. Nowadays they communicate with water-catchment groups, learn about pollution laws, sit at computer terminals and absorb new ideas. But they never lose their grip on the inherited ethics that help them through the turmoils of farm life.

I have to believe I can make a difference in the country. I didn't feel that in the city, where there's a sense of imper-manence and replaceability. Near Scone there's a meeting to discuss matters environmental. We're a loose coalition. We start our get-together by saying what we're thinking, what we're involved in. Most of us express the same sense of being awash in theory, of half knowing things. There's agreement we must embrace our ideas, develop them, live them, if we're going to be true to our word. Our world.

Choice is something country people often don't have. There are very few radio and television stations, for instance – SBS still hasn't found its way to the Upper Hunter. With fewer people around and less choice, you feel more important. It's an illusion but it helps. Less choice makes responsibilities feel bigger. I like that. Mattering matters.

Of more concern than the lack of choice is the lack of

diversity. David Malouf, again in his Boyer Lectures, says, 'You need to believe in the idea of diversity perhaps before you develop an eye for it in the world about you.' It's not just the diversity of species that is shrinking in the bush, it's the whole idea. Throughout Europe the traveller is confronted with a geological layering of cultures, sites that recall the influences of Greeks, Etruscans, Romans, the Moors. But my suggestion to a local committee that we provide booklets on the region's Aboriginal history was met with a mixture of sullen silence and open hostility. Not wishing to ignite a racial debate in an area where One Nation enjoys strong support, I let the matter drop. It was clear that the culture of the Wonnarua people would have to wait. We want one cultural face. When I later suggested we erect a Patrick White monument, as his family lived up the road, a man asked, 'What did he ever do for Gundy?' So our only Nobel Laureate for literature joined the Wonnarua in the outer darkness.

The land itself should define its use: those flats for crops, those hills for trees, etc. But science has changed these assumptions, and by moving water across dry land, by tapping into oases deep underground, adding chemicals and fertilisers, planting new seed varieties, it's possible to grow almost anything anywhere. Think of the rice paddies in the Philippines: who first dreamt of growing rice on almost vertical hillsides? Today these rice paddies are regarded as a triumph of human ingenuity, part of the great Filipino aesthetic. The terraced olive groves of France and Italy made dry dull hills into something beautiful: did anyone tell the farmers that catching water on the hillside diminishes run-off and can be bad for streams?

The difficulty we have in accepting environmental truths comes from being so sheltered from most of them. Television and newspapers may convince us there's some truth in the environmentalists' arguments, but when we drive around the countryside, especially after rain, we see only beauty, growth and life. So where exactly is the mass destruction that we're told is underway across the nation? It's hard to accept that the capacity of land is limited when we're being told we can increase productivity, get more protein, more meat, more this or that. Everything can increase. Life itself. Our population soars. We live longer. Athletes break world records as if the human body knows no limits. But at what price? With what drugs? So a good farmer asks, what price food? Accepting the limitations of the land is the heart of the matter.

The real issue is how to produce food, all kinds of foods, without diminishing our soil and water resources. Biodynamics isn't just about not using chemicals. It's about making the soils of Australia – those particles of dust we see blowing in the wind – into humus producers. Biodynamics is the third way between industrial agriculture and small, lifestyle farms. Like many traditional farmers all over the country who've converted to managing land without chemicals, we believe we've found a better, safer way to grow food.

Ironically, the organic/biodynamic food industry is growing at a time when the world has created a massive bureaucracy to ensure food safety. Food is to be doused, sprayed or irradiated to eliminate any sign of contaminants. It's now deemed 'safer' by the food authorities to have apples sprayed in order to slow down spoilage, even if the approved chemical may depress your nervous system. Many people disapprove of food production becoming industrialised. They want to believe, and rightly so, that the food they're buying and giving to their children is the cleanest, safest food and that its production hasn't polluted the earth. These are the people who buy biodynamic food. They want to be part of what they see as a sustainable future, to contribute to a safer environment.

Elmswood is our opportunity to bring together theory and practice. It is the place where I ask the questions and learn some answers. It is the place where I stop pontificating and simply try and work out a way of making our place a home, a business, an ecosystem. For I know T.S. Eliot is right:

Between the idea
And the reality
Between the motion
And the act
Falls the shadow

Indeed, a very long shadow that fools us into believing we can't make a difference, that the ways of the world are beyond our comprehension and influence, that we can only find comfort in material things and have a good laugh. But in the end we must move on. To borrow Amnesty International's slogan, Better to light a candle than curse the darkness.

I look out the window and see animals grazing on the hills. They depend on me to ensure they are cared for. One minute I'm childless, next minute I have hundreds of calves and lambs and trees under my charge. It makes me think.

In our few spare minutes, usually around midnight, Phillip and I go through the piles of jokes we've collected for an anthology of Australian humour. Phillip's favourite – he thinks it sums up most attributes of rural life – concerns a couple of fencing contractors in northern New South Wales. Having just received their cheque from the cocky, they're debating their next move.

'Think I'll go down to Sinny.'

'Yeah, I hear Sinny's a pretty good place.'

There's a pause.

'What route are you taking?'

'I reckon I'll take the wife. She stuck with me through the drought.'

It's on my mind when I ring Bruce, a local fencer whom I wish we'd known years ago. Fencing is an art. The Horse Paddock must be made safe from the marauding bovines. I want a strong, traditional – and expensive – fence; one wood to three steel posts, five wires, two barbed. In a couple of weeks Bruce defines the space. We walk along his creation, impressed with its evenness, tight wires and strength, feeling the same sense of pride and comfort you feel when you know your actions will protect your child. This irrefutable line has given us a place for our olive cloister. Even before the trees are delivered, this side of the fence feels different.

The Agrowplow is slowly dragged across the contours. The 90-horsepower tractor can only just manage. Rocks are heaved to the ground. The site turns into a gibber hill. The Horse Paddock joins an L-shaped lucerne paddock that wraps around the house to the north. Its 8 hectares have provided tonnes of biodynamic hay and silage every year for our cattle. We hadn't considered planting trees there until we did a soil structure test and decided that 3 metres of alkaline sandy loam, perfectly drained, would probably grow good olives. But to give up lucerne is a big ask. We decide to extend the lucerne in the adjacent paddock, where we strip-graze the pasture to finish cattle for market. It's the best paddock close to the yards, so cattle usually have a few days there before being trucked off. We pull down a few fences and designate about 3 hectares of the lucerne for olives. We do a last cut, then the great iron claws of the deep ripper are dragged behind the tractor, opening up the soil in readiness for planting. However, the lucerne persists, so months later JP goes over it again, just the rows this time, with an attachment to help cut the roots. Once the plants have died, he sod sows Haifa white clover into it. Because we won't be spraying chemicals, we'll need to have a good ground cover to protect the soil. In the early years we'll mulch with the hay we grow between the rows, or with any spoilt hay, which we don't often have now that we make silage.

I can't put it off any longer. The one thing that must be done tomorrow – after feeding the chooks, checking the tanks, booking cattle in for slaughter, paying a few weekly bills and making a large pot of green tea – is decide which olive varieties to plant. If we're to plant this year, they must be ordered immediately. While I've procrastinated, the waiting period for the delivery of young trees has extended to nine months and is lengthening by the day. I print CHOOSE OLIVES on a clean sheet of paper and place it on top of the junk on my desk, put the ingredients into the breadmaker so there'll be a hot loaf in the morning, set the alarm for six and go to bed.

During the past few weeks I've been ringing people more decisive than myself and asking them to explain how and why they arrived at their varietal selection, and I don't always like what I hear. One grower planted a thousand trees because the nursery had them on special, but they're a variety with little oil content. One man thought Paragon was a nice name. And someone else ordered seven varieties because she couldn't make up her mind.

'Good for you. We grew olives in Puglia,' the Italian deli owner said, laughing, when I told him we were planting a grove of our own and I wouldn't be buying his outrageously expensive stuff much longer.

'What kind of oil do *you* want to make, Patrizia?' Why ask me this? What kind? The best kind of course. Wrapping the bottles of imported oils in brown paper, he patiently waited for my considered opinion. Finally, I said in my best Italian, with appropriate gestures, '*Buona, fresca, bellissima.*' He beamed, approving of my ambitions, and suggested two varieties I've never heard of.

An omen: having set my mind on fifteen hundred trees for the first planting, I dreamt we planted the most exquisite trees and they all died. No, we must plant three kinds. Take a bet each way.

They're still making mistakes in the neighbouring vineyards. Recently, whole plantings near here have been ripped up. Grapes don't take as long to produce as olives, but oh, the time and money wasted!

It will be years before we'll really know if what we've planted produces the right type of oil. 'If they're a flop, just saw them off and graft. That's what we're going to do if they all turn out be a disaster,' soothes one eager grower. Graft a multitude of trees? I don't think so.

Should our three varieties ripen together to make harvesting easier? I pass over those varieties claiming to ripen early, exhausted at the mere thought of overseeing a harvest at the end of February when it's so hot all I want to do is lock myself naked in the office with the airconditioner blasting. I toss out those that ripen late as well; June or July is certain to bring frosts. Commonsense tells me that three different harvests will lessen the risk of hail damage, wind damage, insect infestations, wet seasons, dry seasons, or any other imaginable disaster. But will I be able to get the harvest contractor to return three times? If they all ripen together, how will we get them off in time?

Our determination to produce oil vetoes all the pickling varieties. Forget Sevillano, Kalamata, Barouni. Eventually, mechanical harvesting will be essential if we're to make any money, so the olives must fall off the trees easily when shaken. Many don't, according to the manuals. And above all, there's flavour and character to consider.

I flick through *OLIVAE* (a trade magazine put out in three languages by the International Olive Oil Council) and learn that Picual, the most common tree in Spain, is described as being of medium quality, susceptible to peacock spot and verticillium wilt. Why would anyone plant a variety of medium quality?

Cross-checking each variety on my original list – Arbequina, Correggiola, Koroneiki, Mission, Frantoio, Pendulina, Picual, Manzanilla, Verdale – I try to assess if they will survive the cold, have a high oil content, not be prone to disease. My pages of notes begin to look like a mad woman's scribble. Every name gets a question mark after it and eventually a line through it.

In the morning I go downstairs and slice my fresh bread. Clasping a thick chunk with tongs, I toast it over the gas burner. It smells delicious. Adding a sprinkling of salt and oil I munch away, enjoying the knowledge that one day I'll be pouring my own oil over my bread. I read the bottle labels as I eat. The organic oil from Umbria is under six months old and smells of Italy. Sitting alone at the kitchen table, listening to a Vivaldi violin concerto, I try to understand what I like or don't like about each oil. Do they enhance the bread and tantalise the palate? Someone in an old shed in the back streets of an Italian village has decided that this is the oil they'll send out to the world. This is their idea of the good oil. What will mine be?

Loving all things Italian, I mull over the Tuscan trifecta: Correggiola, Leccino and Moraiolo. Why look beyond these three? Why make life complex? Some things are self-evident. The Tuscan blend of olive oil is famous and, many argue, the best in the world. Tuscany is as cold and as hot as Elmswood. There is my answer.

But Moraiolo isn't available in Australia. Leccino is only grown at one nursery, in Western Australia, and there's a two-year waiting list. While Correggiola and Frantoio are often regarded as regional names for the same variety, recent evidence suggests they're different. Research papers contradict each other. Should I order Frantoio or Correggiola?

Frustrated, I phone an olive oil wholesaler. 'What can you tell me about Mission?' 'Which Mission?' he says. 'Californian Mission or Western Australian Mission? The Californian one is good, makes a nice mellow oil.'

Mission had been on the top of my cold-hardy list, but I'd crossed it off. Now it's back on. Uneasily, I order five hundred Californian Mission. A thousand trees to go. Correggiola (even if it is Frantoio) is always described as a rich, savoury, aromatic, distinctive Tuscan oil. I'll order Leccino for the second planting, in two years, but I still need five hundred more now.

I ring a fellow grower who, inspired by research at Mildura where trees have cropped almost 200 kilograms of fruit in a good year, has planted thousands of Manzanilla. 'More fruit, more money,' she says. But that's not always right, think of the orange growers. Manzanilla is the main variety grown in California, where they produce and pickle inedible olives to put on pizzas. Should I condemn the tree because of American bad taste? It's considered a dual-purpose tree, good for pickling, good for oil. The concept of dual purpose bothers me. It's neither this nor that. I like all things to know what they are about. 'But is the oil any good?' I ask.

'It's being sold as a varietal oil, Patrice,' my friend says, as if this proves something.

'Most people are planting Manzanilla,' the nursery tells me. So if we make a mistake we'll be able to share the experience? A bit like the *Titanic*? We'll all go down together?

The final order: Mission, Correggiola, Manzanilla. I have no idea how their oils created on Gundy soil will blend. But then, who does?

As if olives aren't enough, another project emerges. Or rather, re-emerges. It's embarrassing that we've never really completely unpacked, that there are still mysterious boxes branded 'Kent's Removalists' piled at the top of the stairs. Now the homestead is filling with more boxes bursting with books. Two large rooms, intended as bedrooms, have been allocated as libraries and they're completely full, floor to ceiling. So are the auxiliary shelves built on either side of the fireplaces in Rory's room, the spare bedroom and the office. And still the books keep arriving. Add to that boxes of personal papers (Phillip's), various pictures which can't be squeezed onto crowded walls, and statues that are forming queues in the hall, and it's painfully clear we either have to divest ourselves of possessions or build an extension.

I've always travelled light, I favour giving books away and believe public museums serve a useful purpose. But I live with a collector, a man with a genetic predisposition to collect things. Any things. And his greatest pleasure is to waste time ordering and reordering them, arranging his statues like a general his troops. I never know what's going to turn up next.

A typical case: Phillip returns from a shopping expedition in Scone with a couple of old broken drawers once used by printers to hold metallic type. They've been tossed out by the local printer, who after a hundred years has changed technology. Thinking they're marvellous, Phillip nails them to the kitchen and patio walls, then fills them with pieces of broken china, portions of their traditional patterns still showing, and with glass – all found in the garden, or revealed when storms wash away the earth around the chicken coop. Bits and pieces that, until now, he'd tossed into the little wooden boxes that contained the tea we buy in bulk. Unbeknown to me, they were, all along, waiting to be displayed in the discarded drawers from a printery.

Collectors speak their own language. Recently we visited Nundle, where Peter and Judy Howarth have 'collected' all the abandoned shops and empty buildings, turning them into healthy businesses so that the town may live on. At their farm, Wombramurra, we see how Judy has skilfully arranged in the original slab-hut homestead the bits and pieces she's found around the property – old maps of land purchases, battered photographs, shards of pottery, an ancient teddy bear. Phillip is enchanted by the fact that her pottery shards are the same as his, and he's very impressed with the way Judy has arranged her detritus. Peter and I leave them muttering mysteriously to each other.

Rory has inherited the collector's gene, although her collections are of a more disposable nature. She puts nails in jars; pins leaves to cardboard; fills cereal boxes with corks, rocks, butterfly wings; cuts out faces from magazines. There are times when her flotsam seems to fill the entire kitchen.

I, on the other hand, am entirely innocent. I collect only useful things like rubber bands and pieces of string. Our bedroom, at my insistence, remains the only room in the house spared the confusion of collections. There's not a single picture on the cream walls. The view is decoration enough. When Phillip looks longingly at the unbroken vistas of painted plaster, I realise it's time to seriously consider another building.

Occasionally, I yearn for Phillip's mania to end, and for his four daughters, me, and all his friends to be enough. But he has a deep, inexplicable need to surround himself with *things*, not people. It's the things-people-have-made that link him to the world. So that in between the thousands of objects and the tens of thousands of books, my mood fluctuates between feeling privileged and crushed.

Had we bought land without a house, I'd have wanted a stone-and-glass, horseshoe-shaped building with a paved courtyard. But what we're about to build isn't for us to live in, it's merely to accommodate the larval flow of *things*. It will not be a place for eating and sleeping, it will be a folly, a waste of space.

'A bold structure,' Phillip announces.

'But simple,' I add. I query him. Does he see it more as a shed? A garage? A stable? We settle on a barn. Part of the space can store beekeeping equipment, perhaps one corner could be for meat storage. Even better, let's buy a coolroom! But Phillip wants only books and art.

Arguing over materials, style and purpose, we hire architects, only to dispute their plans. Then, sitting around the kitchen table one evening with friends David and Edna, we start looking at photographs of classic farm buildings; we discuss roof angles, the beauty of timbers, the tradition of pole structures, and scribble a few ideas. For the first time a consensus begins to form. The following morning, drowsy in bed, Phillip and I mull over the previous night's conversation and wonder if David, who's a professional painter with a builder's licence and good at everything, might be interested in building our barn. And David and Edna are lying in bed downstairs wondering the same thing. By breakfast, we all agree that David will tackle the task.

David and Edna have been friends of ours for years. They're about to leave the city and move permanently to their farm at Howes Valley, about an hour away, where

David has already built a small pole building, just big enough to sleep and eat in while tackling an entire home. Little do we know, little do they know, that our barn will delay their departure from Sydney and their plans for Howes Valley for years.

David gathers a coil of rope from the back of his ute and transforms into a pale, Pommy, fifty-something cowboy. Twirling his lariat, he forms a loop and jumps in and out of it. It rises up over his head, hovers and glides down his body, to our delight and applause. The dogs bark. Birds laugh. Rory's met Buffalo Bill! Our quiet, unassuming friend is full of surprises. Talking and acting at a civilised, slow pace, he dabbles in many things besides twirling lariats. He plays the bagpipes, is an artisan with leather, and can repair anything with an engine. And he, too, is a collector, his garage overflowing with vintage cars in various stages of disrepair.

Edna is equally skilled with her time and her hands, raising four children with a busy husband. When she stays, the kitchen is always tidy and she whips up pies, breads and cakes in a flash. And any time she's sitting down she's doing something: plaiting baling twine into reins, waxing saddles, knitting beanies, demonstrating French crochet to Rory, or nailing up frames for honey.

It was due to Edna that I became an apiarist. We'd been talking about the way bees danced, about varieties of honey, when Edna thought she knew someone who could give us a foundation hive. She wanted bees too. A few weeks later she arrived with a hive on the back of her ute, the opening stuffed with a rag so the bees couldn't escape. She keeps her hives next to the clothes-line to observe them closely and care for them – like she does her many dogs (and David) – with abundant atten-tion and love.

We're not sure where the barn should be. First we con-sider parts of the garden, but its greenery is too satisfying. We move our thoughts west, amongst a copse of ironbarks. The front will face north, we could include a verandah for twilight reflection.

Weeks pass and drawings are faxed back and forth between David and the farm. Then one weekend he arrives with a balsa-wood model. Placing it proudly on the centre of the table, he lifts the roof to reveal the internal structure. It's everything we hoped it would be. Simple. Pure. Our barn.

Farm disaster tales are like trophies, natural conversation starters. Floods, fires, plagues of rabbits, locusts, prickly pear, they're the meat on the plate. When we arrived here we didn't have any disasters to contribute, so sympathising neighbours supplied us with their own grim versions of Elmswood's history. Soon I didn't want to hear more stories of drowning in the river, suicide off the balcony, sheep living in our downstairs lounge room, violent fathers. At this rate there'd be no room for my optimism.

Fortunately they also told us stories about happier days. Of famous bullock drivers, great musters, historic cattle sales. A woman who's lived in the district for decades knows all about Elmswood's interior decoration, why the red cedar in one bedroom was painted white, and how the heavy velvet curtains, which we've preserved, took days to hang.

For anyone over fifty, stories of riding ponies to school and visiting town just twice a year is a living memory. Life changed when many wooden bridges were erected, cars were bought, women learnt to drive, and access to town became easier. Huge parties, crowded local stores, delicious bakeries and church picnics began to disappear in the fifties.

After hearing so many tales about the farm I begin a file named 'Elmswood History' and jam it with notes, letters and old photos. People lend their scrapbooks filled with cuttings from the local paper about wins at the gymkhana, school choir performances, happy snaps at the races. Phillip writes about Elmswood in his column in the *Weekend Australian* and we get letters from people all over the country who have visited, driven past or owned the place. One letter from Colin Brayshaw of Broken Hill, who left Elmswood in 1938, provides details of a rich life. We start corresponding, and over the years he will send us some thirty pages of memories.

> The main top balcony was blown off twice by cyclone-type winds which left paths of fallen trees about 200 yards wide – the second time when I was on the balcony watching the storm approaching and only saved myself by lunging through the doorway [. . .] During our occupancy the homestead employed a staff consisting of cook, laundry woman and general help, butler, two housemaids, gardener (vegetables) and yardman. The homestead had its own cattle and sheep slaughter yards together with butcher shop [. . .] There were no aborigines on Elmswood during our time except Alice a domestic help sent from a Sydney agency. After a few weeks she left and moved in with a rabbiter camped on the river bank.

What is the history of the local Aboriginal people – the Wonnarua, Kamilaroi, Geawegal, Gringai and Darkinung? I start asking everyone if they know anything about local Aboriginal culture. There isn't any, I'm told. Many local histories of pioneering families start their stories with the day their ancestors arrive. Colin Brayshaw mentions his niece, Dr Helen Brayshaw, author of a book called *Aborigines of the Hunter Valley* (Scone and Upper Hunter Historical Society, 1986), who lived up the road at Miranee, once part of Elmswood. Her book is a precious publication because of its rarity, and from it I learn of James Miller, a member of the Wonnarua tribe, and his book, *Koori: A Will to Win* (Angus & Robertson, 1985). These two books, along with a few archaeological publications, brief mentions in Scone historical monographs and the notebooks of early explorers, are almost the sum total of texts about local Aboriginal culture. And it's depressing reading. After numerous massacres, the first smallpox outbreak in 1789 and the second epidemic in 1829–30, the Hunter Valley tribes were virtually wiped out as early as 1831.

According to Colin Brayshaw, Wilfred Green of Gundy (1890–1976) 'was recognised as the authority on all matters and everyone went to him with their problem, whether it was to do with the law, taxation, health, general guidance or whatever'. All services were granted free. Green also held literary ambitions and recorded that when the Church of England decided to build their church at the site of the Aboriginal camp in 1867, the Aborigines refused to leave. 'The church people,' Colin wrote, 'made use of their knowledge of Aboriginal customs and arranged to have the body of a dead Aboriginal brought into the camp from higher up the river. The tribe left at once, forming a new camp near the foot of Willis's Hill.'

At the end of the nineteenth century some fifty Aboriginal people lived on Crown land beside the Pages River near Gundy. In an 1872 survey of Gundy, a notation says, 'Permission to occupy some of these allotments granted to Billy Murphy.' Mr Murphy was allegedly the recognised leader of the group. Sorry tales of 'half-caste' alcoholics living along the Pages are mentioned, and then one 'makes good' and has his name memorialised in the Roll of Honour for World War I.

The word 'Gundy' means camp. 'Gundy Gundy' means big camp. Folklore has it that below what we call the Seventh Paddock today, where a large waterhole has formed at a bend in the Pages River, the Wonnarua people settled after being forced from the church ground. As we move cattle, it's easy to see how this beautiful place could have once been home to hundreds of Wonnarua people – but then we think that about a lot of places on Elmswood. This land must have been occupied, it's simply too glorious, too aesthetically perfect to have been ignored by Aborigines.

James Miller mentions that the Wonnarua people were possibly the first tribe to accept children of mixed descent and this helped prevent a full genocide. Colin Brayshaw wrote to us about trees on the river's edge below the house having Aboriginal carvings, and there are sketches of the trees in Helen Brayshaw's book. But during floods in 1929 the trees were washed away. How many other engraved trees were felled for timber is now anyone's guess.

Years pass before I call into the Wanaruah Land Council on the New England Highway in Muswellbrook. Freeda Archibald, the young director accustomed to racist remarks and lack of community support for Wonnarua claims to

Crown land, is suspicious of my visit. I ask where important Aboriginal landmarks are and am told that the council doesn't publicise archaeological sites as vandalism is a constant threat. But how can white people learn about the culture if we're never told about it, never shown it? I tell Freeda that as I drive from Sydney to Elmswood I see no evidence of the Aboriginal heritage of the area. She looks at me as if I'm blind. It's all Aboriginal land, she says. Do I need a sign saying ABORIGINAL SITE plastered across the road as evidence? Freeda takes me into another room with a large map on the wall. It's a 1997 National Parks and Wildlife Service map of the Hunter Valley, showing all the known Aboriginal archaeological sites. Between Muswellbrook and Singleton there are a lot of symbols. I'm excited. So this is what I've been driving past all the time, hundreds of important landmarks. Freeda runs her fingers across the map to areas north and east of Scone, past Elmswood and says, 'The reason there're so few marks here is because very little research has been done in these areas.'

It wasn't until 1965 that the Australian Museum conducted its survey of the valley, concluding that 'virtually every side valley contained important relics and probably occupation deposits'.

After years of living here, understanding local Aboriginal culture, the old and the new, remains difficult. It doesn't seep into my life. It's never discussed, never glorified, never celebrated. It's easier to find information about plants at the time of white settlement. Having lived through landmarks like Mabo and Wik, and a referendum on becoming a republic, one day surely I'll grasp, at a deeper level, our early history without feeling ashamed and threatened. Perhaps Rory's generation will pluck from a wider source of memory and anecdote to paint and appreciate indigenous history and culture.

Every morning I open wooden shutters and look out over the lucerne to where two rivers meet. The Isis ends, joining the Pages. I drive over the Pages River every time I leave the property. Phillip enjoys the idea of the Isis, the Egyptian connection intensified by the ibis picking their way across the paddocks. He positions an eighteenth-dynasty mummy case in the hallway. Another next to it, then another. Gradually, bits and pieces from the Nile find their place through all the rooms, and statues of Isis call to the river.

The Isis and the Pages are officially designated 'unregulated streams', to which the adjective 'stressed' has just been added. You'd think that where two rivers meet there'd be a visible increase in the flow, but there isn't, except when there's a flood. In dry times each of the rivers disappears beneath its bed, surfacing in the occasional precious pool. Year by year we've seen the combined flow slowing. Too many people upstream are taking too much water from the Isis and the Pages. Now algae, as thick as pea soup, arrives earlier and leaves later. Everyone comments on it. The river is struggling but there's no consensus on how we are to save it.

A friend phones with more bad news: there's algae at the head of a creek, yet the surrounding paddocks haven't been supered in years. How has it happened? he asks. Someone else has an answer: previous owners have tossed superphosphate in the dams to encourage water plants, in order to feed their fingerlings. We are the disease that afflicts the land, rivers and streams. Can we become the doctors? Can we agree on a diagnosis and prescribe a treatment?

At a meeting called to discuss our river, a sixth-generation landowner stands up and demands we dam it. 'I'm sick of seeing all that water flowing down the river during floods,' he says. The representative from the Department of Land and Water Conservation responds tersely, 'There'll never be another dam built in this state. Rivers need flooding.' In any case, governments aren't in the business of building assets these days, they're into selling them.

Booklets circulating amongst water-user groups state the obvious. Rivers need water if they are to stay healthy, but historically water hasn't been allocated to the stream itself. The debate is now shifting to exactly how much water a river needs in order to survive, and who will give up their allocation. The winners at present are the old-timers who have huge irrigation entitlements and are thinking of quitting agriculture. Their licences are worth gold and are being energetically traded.

In the early part of 1998, when the river was bone-dry and everyone was panicking, the Pages and Isis Water Users Association was formed, but it lost its energy as soon as it rained. After a couple of one-day floods there was no apparent need to worry about the river. We all know that finally we'll be forced to *do* something, because when self-regulation fails, as it always does, the government is called in to umpire. Rain or no rain, we need to come to a deeper understanding of what the Isis and the Pages need.

If we were to have a meeting now, with all the water users from our section of the river coming together to discuss the issue, I can image what they'd say. Let's start with that most elite sport, polo. The local polo club manager would argue that polo has cultural significance to the area, is an important part of the local social calendar, and unites people passionate about horses and balls (of both the hitting and dress-up kind). The polo field must be kept green, cut, and looking its best *at all times.*

Years ago, when it was common for shires to do such things, Scone decided to give the district a theme. Now we're Scone, Horse Capital of Australia. Beef and sheep are still the main local rural industries, although that too may be changing.

Downstream from the polo field, the most visible members of the marketing plan are the racehorse studs. Breeders of million-dollar thoroughbreds and Randwick winners, they raise their eyebrows at the polo push. Polo is, after all, only recreational. Racing, on the other hand, is a billion-dollar industry, leading to a huge investment in the area and significant employment. One stud has sixty people on its payroll. Furthermore, many studs are public companies with 'an obligation to their shareholders', so they keep the sprinklers going only for the sake of appearances. All that investment must look good *at all times*.

Many small horse studs without the fancy fencing and grand entrances demand they not be disadvantaged because of size. How can they grow as a business without lots of water? So they too claim the right to pump water *at all times*.

The lucerne growers produce a thirsty crop deemed essential for the horse industry, so they pour the water on even when it's raining. Some lucerne varieties grow in winter and can be harvested *at all times*.

The local dairy adviser tells me that the dairies of the Upper Hunter are some of the most productive modern rural enterprises in the country. Our local builder recently built a new spandangled one. No expense spared. But cows have to eat *at all times*; otherwise, how can they produce milk?

The long-time cattle and sheep breeders have been using water for seven generations and it is their historical right to continue to do so. Why should they suffer because the region is diversifying? While dams catch run-off, farmers pump out of the river to tanks that in turn feed troughs for stock. Cattle and sheep drink a lot. Some water must be left for them *at all times*.

(Meanwhile, further up the valley at Ellerston, on the Pages Creek, Kerry Packer has installed a professional, Greg Norman-designed golf course alongside his many polo fields. These need water *at all times*.)

And lower down the food chain, people living on rural residential blocks claim they shouldn't be penalised just because they're not full-time farmers. For they have what's called a riparian right – that is, an entitlement to pump from the river for stock and domestic use and to irrigate 2 hectares of land. They're not trying to make a living off their land, they just want it to look good *at all times*.

Gundy is a village without town water and most residents have pumps in the river. For some, these are their only water supply. They need water *at all times*. There's a loose agreement that the river must always flow to Gundy. It doesn't. People upstream, determined to get their last drip, aren't driving down to Gundy to check the flow.

We're using a small part of our water allocation for olives. While they mightn't die without irrigation, they won't be productive. They need access to water *at all times*.

So who will decide who should get this limited resource? Whose priorities will take precedence in the twenty-first century? Will councils be under such financial pressure that they'll do anything to lure more ratepayers and development, regardless of the environmental consequences? Ignoring the fact that rivers are already dying or dead?

A group of us prepare to confront some subdivision plans for local farms. One man pins a large map of Australia to the wall. It dramatically differentiates between the green fringe on the eastern seaboard and the vast brown hinterland.

'This is where most people live,' he says, pointing to the green. 'And it's also the most productive land. This is where we raise our food and we're covering it with suburbs and car parks.' His stick hits the brown bits. 'We're farming in arid regions and creating deserts. And we talk about sustaina-bloody-bility!'

We all need to look at that map of Australia. If farmers and people moving into the rural sector to live on the land won't face the issues, who will?

Irrigation systems are mathematical equations. Before the first tree can be planted in our olive grove, the whole site must be surveyed and a detailed plan prepared.

I phone Owen at Scone, who's been selling us joiners and pipes for years, and he arranges for Alain, a charming Frenchman who's designed irrigation for groves in Jordan, to visit. I explain what we want and he works out how to get the water to the site and what size pipe and filters will be needed. Eventually Alain's plan, meticulously hand-written, arrives. I book a trench digger to lay the mains and sub-mains, then it's back to Owen to order the various fittings and pumps.

Checking the final order, Owen asks, 'Any cables underground?'

Oh! Why hadn't I thought of that?

Hidden beneath Elmswood, from one end of the property to the other, are countless kilometres of tele-communication cables. When the cattle chew down the grass, cement casings with 'Telstra' etched into them appear; sometimes hooves break the lids, revealing a mess of wires, and sometimes those cables are hoisted high above a gully on thin, leaning wooden poles. Our farm provides a shortcut linking Moonan Flat, Ellerston and beyond to the wider world. 'Cut 'em luvvy and you won't be drinking at Moonan again!' says a technician checking them one day. But where exactly are these underground cables? He can't tell me, but promises to come out with a gadget to test a couple of likely areas. Rattling off details of storms, accidents and gardening extensions that have made his life a misery over the years, he drives to where he knows for absolute certain that some cables are buried. But when he arrives he's not absolutely sure. New wires are added to the spaghetti whenever a new property is developed. It's all ad hoc after ad hoc. The current layout is anyone's guess.

I remember a faded sign on a fence near where the olives will be. It says TELECOMMUNICATION WIRES IN THIS VICINITY. A vicinity is a big place out here. I phone the new, getting-ready-to-be-privatised Telstra from Owen's office. Could someone please come out and locate the cables? Telstra doesn't supply that service any more, I'm told. Silly me. Telstra is shedding staff to make more profits so it can pay the shareholders of the future, so now they send maps in the mail. I explain to a cheery girl where we live and she promises to fax me a map straight away. I go home relieved that everything is arranged, but when I get there, no fax is waiting. So I ring again, this time to hear a recorded message that all lines are busy and I've been placed in a queue. Finally I'm told, by another girl, 'It's not my fault you didn't get the fax.' Never is.

'But I need to know straight away because I've got the trench digger arriving tomorrow,' I tell her. As if she cares.

What finally arrives is the new Telstra policy explaining that all landowners are fully responsible if they accidentally dig up a cable. The whole bill will be ours. I'm on the phone again. 'But I don't know where the cables are. Tell me!'

In the morning the trencher is parked on the road. Joe the operator is looking over his shoulder at the Telstra cable sign. He's dug up cables before and knows what havoc it causes. I have visions of everyone east of Elmswood being without a phone, including an eighty-year-old woman who lives alone. Judging by the amount of time we now wait for a Telstra service call, she could be without a phone for days. After more arguments with Telstra, and still no map, I look up at the sky and realise it's going to rain. We can't afford to waste another day. Be bold. Take a risk. My fingers are crossed. I take a deep breath and Joe sinks the trencher into the black soil.

I'm too nervous to watch. The machine, turning out back soil as it goes, moves slowly across the paddock. The only thing he cuts is a water pipe to a trough. Phew! What a tense day. As Joe drives the trencher onto the truck to go home, it buckets down for half an hour. Someone was on our side today.

I go to bed thinking we must have on permanent file a proper map with all the cables marked. I waste more time trying to get such a map covering about 2000 hectares, but I never succeed. All I get sent is a vague diagram of one small area. So while landholders are responsible for damaging cables, we're meant to guess where they are.

Two years later, when new cables need to be laid on an adjoining property, the contractors pay us a visit hoping we have plans of the cables across Elmswood because Telstra has none on record.

It's been an exceptionally warm autumn and now the ground is only slightly moist. JP and I wander across the old lucerne paddock to check on preparations for our grove. It's all coming together. We'll be planting the trees soon.

Autumn brings the best of times. The lower sun, the lessened heat, the cool nights and the need to chop wood again. Neighbours speak of feeling twice as energetic. People are riding longer, gardening more, smiling. Light changes the textures. Leaves don't appear starved for water. The land relaxes. I relax.

Year after year, hundreds of raucous sulphur-crested cockatoos fill the *Celtis occidentalis* trees around the house, snipping the fine twigs and light branches. They are ruthless, savage pruners, leaving the trees all but bare before any leaf has time to turn yellow. But this year they haven't appeared.

My office overlooks the upstairs verandah and is curtained in golden leaves. It's like a treehouse, and Rory could simply step off the balcony into the branches. I must get the tree surgeon to cut them back. The gentle winds are allowing the leaves to linger.

Instead of cockatoos causing havoc, currawongs have arrived. We've been reading about them, Rory and I. Two weeks earlier, Phillip and I gave her a fine edition of Robert Gray's book *Lineations* (Duffy and Snellgrove, 1996) for her birthday, and the first poem is called 'Currawongs'.

One bird perches on my window ledge and aggressively taps the glass. Its head is fierce. As Gray puts it:

...The eye, barely capsulized

in its split pod, has a rind of poisonous yellow around
a blackly-shining, opaque
blight. It is watching every movement in the air, on the
*   ground,*
as if it's all a card stake ...

They're an unnerving species with a threatening, whistling chorus. And in addition to young wrens, they eat olives.

To make planting easier we decide to tickle the weeds out of the rows one last time with the Agrowplow. The contraption is 4 metres wide, has seven tines and leaves the paddock neatly striped. Brown stripe for planting, green stripe for walking. Yet I shout, 'Get off the soil,' when a friend begins to cross the paddock to meet me. I dread soil compaction.

Down on my knees I fossick amongst the greenery, hoping the white clover oversewn into the old stand of lucerne has already germinated. The more I look, the more I find. Biodynamic farmers have a great affection for clovers, relying on them to fix nitrogen in the soil. A grower in Italy told me, 'You'll never be able to grow good olives unless you add abundant quantities of artificial nitrogen.' I look at our clover, knowing it's helped keep our pastures going year after year, without the need to add anything artificial.

Next we lay the lateral pipes along each row and connect them to the sub-mains. We decide to bury the pipe (less chance of accidents) and just have thin, flexible spaghetti tube connected to drips at each tree. The rows are 350 metres long. We unwind the 19-millimetre pipe, roll it down each row, then drag it a little more, a little more. Finally, to reach the end, I'm like Santa Claus, hauling it over my shoulder as if it's the ultimate present. I'm leaning forward so much my chin could hit the dirt. How can such a thin pipe be so heavy? I've seen a pipe unwinder at Owen's. I phone him and ask to borrow it. Why didn't I think of it yesterday?

This isn't the fun part. I want to get to the climax, putting trees in the ground, but somehow I get through the days of preparation. I pay for impersonating Santa – unknown muscles begin to ache. It hurts to wash the dishes. And I'm coughing.

Once the pipe is laid along each row, it's fed into a layer, an apparatus that saves hours of digging. JP drives the tractor along the row, slowly, gingerly, trying to keep a straight line, which is made more difficult by the need to look back over his shoulder to check the pipe. I stumble behind the huge tractor tyres, which are on the outside of the ploughed row, to make sure the pipe doesn't get buried too deeply.

The following morning Phillip and I bundle up the cane stakes and begin to peg out. The rows are to be 8 metres apart, the trees separated by 5 metres – the new standard layout. Old-timers claim this is too close. 'Olive trees sing to the sun,' they insist. Others say they're not close enough, that modern production has to maximise the ratio of trees to hectares, otherwise profits won't be possible. Despite anxieties over the layout, I've decided that 8×5 it's to be. Two hundred and fifty trees to the hectare.

This area is a strip of sandy loam running east–west. To make the most of the sunshine we plant alternately, so that, viewed from above, the trees won't create a square, but a diamond pattern. We measure the first row and peg it with ease. No arguments. But by the time we start the second row we realise that this flat area isn't flat at all.

I remember a fellow olive grower telling me she had her paddock laid out with lasers. Now I know why. What appears balanced to the eye isn't necessarily. We move the stakes back and forth, until we finally agree that it's better for the stakes to look right rather than actually be right. By the end of the eleventh row, looking like an archer with a quiver of huge arrows, Phillip is pegging on his own.

Now should be the time to plant, but the days have been so warm that the earth has dried. Despite JP's last ploughing, when I try to dig a hole my muscles scream. I kick the soil. The top is dust. Beneath it's like rock. We connect the long aluminium irrigation pipes up, get the big river pump roaring and give the whole area a soak. The dust settles. The soil darkens. The clover jumps. The worms rise. It smells good. Now, at last, we're ready.

The morning is perfect – warm, windless, quiet. In the afternoon, a cool breeze. Once we start, a rhythm is set; the planting happens quickly. I want to savour this time. We will never again *begin* to plant our grove. Phillip says he feels like a slave and imitates Paul Robeson's rendition of 'Old Man River'. If he wasn't a writer, he could have been a singer. All is going to schedule, we should finish the first stage by Easter.

We're so keen to get started that we change our strict Saturday routine and decide to delay reading the morning newspapers until the afternoon. I pack water and food into a basket so we won't need to return to the kitchen, and Phillip, Rory, I and the dogs climb into the Gator and take off.

There are many machines I could live without but the Gator isn't one of them. This two-seater, six-wheeler, all-terrain vehicle with a tip tray at the back for rocks, tools or weeds is what every woman on a farm needs. Hurling hay bales into a four-wheel drive is difficult, just that little bit too high, but it's relatively easy in this. I move the Gator down the row and suddenly Molly is yelping. Why? I look down impatiently – silly dog. But she doesn't stop. The yelp gets louder and ricochets off the shearing shed.

Dropping the watering can and rushing over, Rory shouts, 'Mum, you've run over Molly!' Have the big soft Gator tyres rolled right over her? I bend down to pick her up, she snaps at my hands and won't let me touch her.

Ignoring the biting, Phillip snatches her and clasps his fingers around her jaw to stop her going him. We've lost two dogs to cars, was this going to be the third? We pile back into the Gator and head for the house. Molly is now wriggling so much that I think she can't have broken anything.

'Ring the vet,' Rory demands.

'It's nothing serious. She can still walk. There's only a slight limp,' I say as I lock her in the laundry.

Rory hates me abandoning Molly to the clothes baskets and ironing board and insists on being locked in with her. An hour passes and Molly looks a little worse. 'Ring the vet, Mum! Go on! Molly's going to *die*.'

I ring the vet. I explain what happened. What I think I did. He asks, 'Can she stand up?' 'Yes.' 'What colour are her gums?' Rory checks. Pink. 'Good, if they were white she'd have internal bleeding.' The vet concludes she's pulled a muscle, but we have to keep her in the laundry to let it heal.

'For how long?'

'Probably for two weeks. More if the dog's difficult.' Molly is difficult.

'I'm staying with her, Mum. I'll sleep here *all* night. I'll be a good nurse.'

At some stage in the afternoon Phillip and I go back to the olive grove, exhausted. The drama with the dog has taken the enjoyment out of the planting. We quit early and pack up.

Phillip lights a comfort fire. We don't need the heat as

much as the soothing, dancing light. I place food – fruit, nuts, cheese and homemade bread and honey – on a platter for dinner. Rory appears for a few minutes to eat, and disappears back into the laundry.

At around ten o'clock Phillip returns from checking Molly and the river pump. He says, 'There's been an accident.'

'Another one?'

'The Mazda wasn't in the garage. I thought it was stolen, but then I found it. On top of the olive trees.'

'On *top* of?'

'It must have rolled out of the garage.'

I race out with the torch and there it is, exactly as Phillip said, parked on top of hundreds of crushed trees, delivered a few weeks ago, waiting innocently to be planted.

Suddenly, I have visions of them all mixed up, never to be correctly identified again. Walking through a grove in Tuscany a few years back, I noticed a particularly strong, vibrant tree. The sort that sings out, I'm glad I'm planted here! But the owner couldn't tell me for sure what kind it was. The more I asked for specifics about his varieties, the more evasive he became. 'No one wants to tell you any-thing,' a friend says. 'The Italians want to keep it all a secret.' But it wasn't that at all. Italians are such generous people. The man simply didn't know. What he did know was that he had a mixture of Italian varieties in his thousand-tree hillside. So need I worry? A mix of trees is better than nothing.

I don't really want to spend Sunday repotting a few hundred trees, but life on a farm is never what you expect. Many remain in their pots, despite the crush of the wheels, but look so battered we decide we better get on with the job and redo the lot.

By late Sunday Phillip is on a plane to Perth where he has to give a speech to school teachers. I wish I had a speech to give. Better that than a locked-up crying dog, an overanxious five-year-old nurse and hundreds of trees to plant.

Word is out. Friends telephone. 'Could I come and plant an olive tree?' they ask. No one offered to help with the Chinese elms near the entrance, or the eucalypts up the drive, or the she-oaks along the river, or the honey locusts along the road, but planting an olive tree is different. Friends don't see it as work, a challenge to the shoulders, a strain on the knee caps – you're not planting a tree, but an ideal. Olives have become a multicultural link, an acknowledgement of the Mediterranean in our culture. Like pasta and basil and bocconcini before, now the olive brings us together. Once we sat around the kitchen with a mortar and pestle, taking turns to mash the basil and pine nuts. Now people ask to have the spade passed to them. They want to get back to basics, beginnings; they want to plant.

Yes, come! Soon friends arrive from all over the place to

help. Occasional visitors like Brett, Peter and Chris, and regular ones like Gideon, who is trying to produce an animated television series. Film matters take time to develop, like olive groves. He arrives with electronic gizmo in hand, voice mail linked. Thankfully his mobile doesn't work in the paddock (our hills protect us from many things), so he keeps scurrying back to the kitchen to check for messages.

Sergio drives up from Sydney for a day. He's Italian, with fantasies of having his own grove. Share ours, I'd suggested. In the morning light we plan the day's planting. Yesterday's rain has left the ground gluggy. Five hundred trees wait to be planted, thin, spindly things tied and dependent on the stake, not much thicker than a kitchen skewer. Sergio is daunted. Planting one tree is a symbolic act, planting hundreds is hard work. So Sergio puts on his management hat and starts to get bossy. Here is a man used to commanding respect from obedient employees. How will we tackle this? he asks. Gideon and I look up grinning. 'Let's do a row each,' I suggest.

'Bad work practice. We should each have a set job, assembly-line style, and move down the row,' insists Sergio.

That probably would be more efficient, but I want ritual. 'We'll only plant once,' I say (little did I know), 'so let's enjoy it.'

To make a point I take an early tea break and, leaning back on the thick tyre of the Gator, legs outstretched, I slowly munch fruit and biscuits. But Sergio and Gideon form their short assembly line and after only two hours Sergio is exhausted, though he won't admit it. Only eight more hours till sunset.

I take a look at the trees they've planted and I'm not happy. Fellow olive growers have had some unhelpful help, with trees dying as a consequence of clumsy planting, so I call a halt to the assembly line and delegate jobs. Dig holes. Water. Spread old lucerne hay as mulch. Connect the spaghetti tube to the laterals. I'm the only one with permission to actually place a tree in the ground, but, yes, you can tie the tree to the stake with a staple gun and plastic tape.

Sergio's retreat to Sydney makes way for Sam, the thirteen-year-old son of Susan, who used to be my booker for modelling jobs in New York. He's at school in Singapore and now he's holidaying here. Farm life is new to Sam. He doesn't instinctively know what to do. After a tree explodes in a lightning hit, Gideon offers to remove a massive branch from the road. Tying the chainsaw securely to the back of the four-wheel bike he suggests Sam climb on and go along for the ride. It's at the far end of the property and the trip will take at least three hours. With Sam being an insulin-dependent diabetic, I'm about to refuse permission, but seeing the excitement on his face I reluctantly agree, lest in years to come the farm visit be an unhappy memory. 'Mum, do you remember that time you made me spend a fortnight with that witch in Australia?'

Anyway, Sam has just eaten and taken insulin so he should be fine. But while they're disappearing in a cloud of dust I realise he hasn't taken his little safety pack. His mother told me he must *always* have it with him, so I start worrying, then panicking. Every minute feels like an hour. What will I tell Susan? That I let her only child go bouncing around on a four-wheel bike without his life-support system? After all the notes about diabetes she's faxed and emailed me. After all she's said on the phone. I won't be able to live with myself if anything has happened. Gideon will have no idea what to do.

Then I start worrying about an accident with the chainsaw. JP is mustering cattle kilometres away, so I can't send him after them. And if I go out searching, I won't be back in time to meet the school bus. I'll ask Margaret to collect Rory. But her phone doesn't answer. I phone neighbour one, neighbour two, neighbour three. No answers. Finally, I can't contain myself any longer; I reread all the diabetes notes, pack food, sugar bars, his testing kit and insulin, and take off.

About 5 kilometres out, Gideon and Sam come zooming down the track, flying over the creek, bouncing over the bumps, driving way too fast and loving every minute of it. They're laughing until they see me, old worry wart up on top of the hill.

'It was a bugger of a tree to cut up,' Gideon says.

'Oh.'

They don't notice I've pulled half my hair out.

'What are you doing here anyway? Isn't the bus due?'

'Christ!'

As I race down the hill I see the bus disappear along the road. Rory's standing on the bridge, peering into the water looking for eels.

'Oh hi, Mum. No eels today.'

Next morning in the kitchen, with Beethoven blaring, Gideon positions the telephone beside him so he feels secure and starts attaching drippers to the ends of tubes. He looks at the phone longingly. Friends are always calling. Will he be back for coffee at the Tropicana tomorrow? Did he read that article in the *New York Review of Books*? What about Mary splitting up with Don? On and on and on. But this morning, apart from the triumphant ending of the *Pastoral* symphony, all is quiet.

I teach Sam how to drive the Gator so he can help in the grove. He drives up and down the rows, dropping off a hare guard at each tree. Is he enjoying himself? 'Look at him,' JP says. 'He's having the time of his life!' What can JP see that I can't?

Adolescent boys are hard nuts to crack. The few who've worked here over the years belonged to another species. Will Sam tell his mother he had fun? Or that I made him work too much? At night he opens thick textbooks to study for an entrance examination for a raft of Ivy League high schools. Sam's literacy is impressive and as we quiz each other I realise I'm not Ivy League. (Back home Sam will sail through the test and end up in the Iviest of them all, Phillip's Academy at Andover.)

Between books he contemplates a far more important question: whether to cut the thick blond hair that falls to his shoulders and covers much of his face. 'Are you sure?' I ask him, knowing it's an act of defiance and that many will object. 'Absolutely.' All that's left to decide is whether he'll go for a number one or a number two. Decisions, decisions.

Nineteen-year-old Alex arrives from Brisbane, where he's been studying information technology. He's got a flat-top with blond streaks and Sam considers the look. Last year Alex designed software for us to keep tabs on our cattle, now he's going to lock himself in the dining room and create an olive database. He says, grinning with excitement, 'File Maker Pro is a relational database, Patrice, perfect for the job.' Really? That's good. Alex first came here as an eight-year-old with his mother Lyn so he could run wild, chase chooks and sheep and fall off the haystack. I met Lyn in the early eighties when we spent three intense years studying herbal medicine with Dorothy Hall. Now Lyn runs a successful practice in Queensland, and I mix herbs for animals. Coincidentally, Alex's father was a jackeroo on our property twenty years ago. Farms intertwine lives. Now Alex, not unlike his father all those years ago, rides a horse or bike across the hills; gets to know the same bends in the roads, the river and windmills. I want all our friends to see Elmswood as their place too. There's more than work to share.

People are sleeping all over the house. I collect eggs, pick vegies, make soups, bake breads, and fill bowls with feijoas to satisfy so many appetites. When I need a break from outside, I sit with Alex and gaze at the computer screen.

In Sydney a few weeks earlier I'd struggled through a two-day course on File Maker Pro, and now I give my notes to Alex. What took me hours to dimly grasp he gets instantly. Fiddling with the keyboard, he interrupts his silent concentration with cries of, 'Yes! Wow! Fantastic!' and wants to add more bits and pieces to our original design.

'But I don't *need* to know that,' I keep saying.

'But you might, so let's put it in.'

'I'll never remember how to retrieve it.'

'You can email me if you have a problem.'

Scripts and buttons are calculated. This file goes into this, into that, backwards and forwards. I'll be able to know everything about the grove as long as I feed mountains of data into the system.

'Why don't you record info on every tree, like you do with every cow and calf?'

'No, Alex. No! I'm not a computer nerd yet. I want to go outside sometimes.'

Alex departs happily for university, leaving me elated, exhausted, clear-headed and confused. I can now calculate fruit–oil percentages and compare them on the basis of variations in season, temperature, water, wind. This little metal contraption will help me succeed in my venture, but I shudder at Bill Gates's declaration that speed will be the defining aspect of business in the new century. I don't want life to get any faster. I close the laptop.

Sam decides on a number two. What will his mother say now?

The four of us, Phillip, Rory, Sam and I, complete with luggage, crowd into the car and head for Sydney. We've got to put Sam on his flight to Singapore. I know I looked at the tickets at some stage and Sam's father faxed me confirming the flight. But trouble looms.

I don't know how it happened, but we're sitting around the house in Paddington sipping coffee, chatting, reading the papers, when I feel a sense of dread. I recheck Sam's ticket. His plane is leaving now. At this very minute. I rush to the phone and ring the airport.

'Is the flight delayed?'

'No.'

'Can you hold it?'

'No.'

'We'll be there in fifteen minutes.'

'You should have been here an hour ago.'

Phillip and I have a huge row.

'For God's sake! Sam has to do his entrance exams in Singapore!'

Thankfully other planes will leave for Singapore that day. Is anything more exhausting than an argument?

Back at the farm with a worsening cough, I plan the week ahead. Now Rory has an ear infection and is home from school again. The kindergarten year might be a time to learn the ABC but it's also time to catch every conceivable bug. There are two sorry faces that greet me the next morning, mine in the mirror and Rory's in the bedroom.

At Elmswood we've become addicted to audio cassettes. Phillip will listen to Kenneth Branagh reading Pepys' diaries on his 300-kilometre trip up to Sydney and to Lauren Bacall reading Dorothy Parker's short stories on the way back. If we're driving together I'll give Rory a headset and *Just William* to give us an hour's peace. And when she's sick, I pile her doona with options – *The Muddle Headed Wombat, The Railway Children, Alice in Wonderland, The Magic Pudding*. Jack London's *Call of the Wild*.

I decide to spend the day inside with Rory, and opt for music – Peggy Glanville-Hicks. But it's hard to listen when I can't stop coughing.

I ring Bruce, our favourite fencer. But he's booked up for months, so I'm forced to hire someone else to divide one big paddock into three. Bad mistake. Within weeks his shoddy workmanship has strainer posts lifting and gates awry. Then, to my utter astonishment and outrage, a whole section collapses. It literally flops flat on the ground. The cattle get hopelessly mixed.

Things aren't much better in the olive grove. A month has passed and we still haven't finished the first section. Some trees need new stakes, others hare guards, mulching or tying up. And two rows still need trees.

Opening the blinds at daybreak one morning I'm horrified to see rabbits hopping around the grove. One, two, and then a third. A fourth is actually lifting a hareguard and is nibbling at a tree. I phone Keith, begging him to come immediately and set traps. Patiently, before sunset, Keith wanders around the place looking for recent diggings in order to decide exactly where to set the ten traps dangling over his shoulder. He wants to show me how to do it, but I don't even like setting mousetraps.

The dogs are excited. When I call them they run off. Rory and I chase them, leash them, and lock them in the laundry, calling out to Keith, 'All clear. You can start now.' He begins to scoop out a hollow, brushing away any pebbles that could prevent the trap from snapping shut completely. He bangs in the peg with his setter, making sure it's firm, then opens out the jaws and sets it with his hands – although most people do it with their foot – and rests a short stick under the plate so it won't go off. He lays a neatly cut piece of newspaper about 10×7 centimetres across the plate and sprinkles dirt over the trap for camouflage. Finally, delicately, he removes the stick.

I carefully open the laundry door to feed the dogs and before I know it Molly has escaped and I'm screaming that she's out. In a second she's set off the trap below our bedroom. Yelp, yelp. Miraculously she's not hurt.

'She'll never go down that burrow again,' says Keith.

I think about the dog in my arms and all the worry she's caused over the years. Rory gets some baling twine and we tie her to the leg of the kitchen table.

The next morning, Keith checks the traps. Most have been set off but foxes have chewed the catches. All except one big juicy specimen. 'Do you want it?' Keith asks.

'Yes please.'

Skinning it in a flash he shows me a gland near the tail. 'You've got to remove it, otherwise it'll smell awful.' He gouges it out with a quick flick of his pocketknife and hands me tonight's dinner. Usually I bake bunnies with wine and mustard, but tonight I'll make a pie. A revenge pie.

Front-page news is about an outbreak of whooping cough. Next day I go to the doctor.

'Sounds like it,' says the doctor as I demonstrate my whoop. He hands me a prescription.

I take the antibiotics and get a migraine. The cure is worse than the disease. Weeks pass and while I whoop day and night, six people I know go to hospital with pneumonia. I go back to the doctor.

'Could be farmer's lung,' he says. 'From breathing in dust.'

'Like hay dust?' I ask.

'Yeah. You been around hay?'

'Putting hay around a few hundred trees does tend to put me into close proximity.'

'Any mould on the hay?'

'Sometimes.'

'Do you wear a mask?'

'No.'

'Wear a mask or *don't do it*. And have a rest.'

Rest? Sounds like good advice but how do you do that? JP has to finish planting stage one on his own.

We move our attention to stage two. The area for this, alongside the shearing shed, has the heaviest soil. We weren't going to plant here, but after visiting groves in Tuscany and seeing olives growing in clay that potters could toss on a wheel, we decide this patch of gently sloping black basalt warrants a 300-tree experiment. Our small flock of sheep graze here on spring afternoons and occasionally we cut the pasture for hay. Otherwise it's been left to the kangaroos.

Keith has been helping in the garden for a few hours each week. Now it's time to recruit him for the olive grove.

All hands on deck. JP and Keith will peg out together, I explain the layout and return to the mountain of paperwork in the office. At dusk, I check the day's progress and realise something is strangely not right. I'd given JP the starting point from which all trees would flow, and it was wrong. In my mind's eye the rows were balanced against a new fence, whereas they should have been balanced against the curve of the road. How could I have got it so wrong? It looks discordant, as if we've stuck stakes in the ground at random.

I phone JP and arrange a site inspection for the morning. We agree it must be changed. JP and Keith pull the stakes up and begin again. This time it's perfect, and when the following week an olive grower from Spain visits, the first thing he says is, 'How balanced this looks.' And it does. The stakes form a criss-cross pattern as harmonious as a madrigal. As the setting sun casts long shadows from the stakes I wish we could keep them as a permanent installation, like an artwork. Forget the olive trees. This mathematical purity, providing pattern and diminishing perspective, is worth the effort. Tomorrow we will begin to plant here, and soon some trees will lean ever so slightly out of line, a few will stunt, others surge, and the beauty and clarity of the staking will be forgotten.

A little untidiness, please. The desire for order has a dark and dangerous side, as I discover when walking around Jenny and Brad's grove, a few hours' drive west from here, listening to them apologising for the mess. They planted ten thousand trees in an old cow paddock and left them to survive with an inadequate irrigation system, and the weeds have won the battle. A clump of burr here and there, thistles to climb over, grass choking the hare guards. To reassure my hosts I say, 'Neat farms make me think their owners hate sex.' It's a comment that most would laugh at, but these new olive growers look worried. Does their grove suggest sexual excess? As we march up and down the rows, trying to avoid being spiked, I become increasingly conscious of saying the wrong thing. After I leave, Brad opts for censorship and sprays herbicide. But he still thinks he'll become an organic farmer.

Is neatness a natural human condition? In Aboriginal culture, when food was from plants and animals instead of cans and packets, everything was biodegradable and there was no need to waste time putting things in their place or worrying about litter. Now everything must be ordered. This grass here. That clover there.

When I see neatness, I see waste. There is no waste in nature. The neat farm is one where huge amounts of energy and poison are wasted on keeping it so. The neatness fetishists in our district demand the colour green, especially during a golden summer, so they waste water accordingly.

Civilisation demands formality and structure, abhors a natural jumble, but on a farm this is an excuse to pollute. Earth longs to have things grow in it. Poisons long to eliminate. May the absurd pursuit of excessive neatness be put to rest one day. My favourite image of this disease is a man I once saw in western New South Wales who was mowing the tall grass at his grid with a push mower, at around midday in February when the mercury was over 40 degrees.

Neatness comes at an unacceptably high price. When I see farms with bare earth beneath their fence lines, I know it's due to a quick squirt of a herbicide. In a 1999 edition of *Agriculture Today*, published by the New South Wales Department of Agriculture, there were no less than twelve stories on how best to use this chemical for that problem. One, accompanied by a selection of photos, told of 'agribusiness staff' meeting at Orange (farmers didn't meet, only agribusiness staff met) to learn how to identify weeds at an earlier stage so that they could use chemicals more effectively. With such extensive government endorsements, why do chemical companies need marketing campaigns at all?

Every chemical application is a cry for neatness. Every farmer using a chemical is saying, while they're spraying, 'I'm caring for my patch without consideration of the ecosystem.' The act of spraying is at the end of a long line of damaging acts. Design, manufacture, transportation are all part of the cycle of pollution. Yet poisoning is an accepted, expected farming practice. With the exception of medicinal herbs, every crop, every rural enterprise embraces some form of poisoning. Check the costings of any agricultural enterprise, and chemicals top the list. Take Cattlecare, the name of the beef industry's latest quality-assurance program, set up by the industry after repeated contamination scares. TAFE runs training courses on this program and 20% of the lessons are about how to handle chemicals properly. I've not met any agronomist trained at an agricultural college who isn't advising chemical usage. Cashed-up landowners are told not to buy more land but to improve what they have, that is, add polluting, inorganic fertilisers to their soils and keep their property neat by spraying herbicides. Some improvement.

Chemical manufacturing is controlled by a handful of multinational companies. One of the biggest, Monsanto (now merged with Pharmacia), is to farming what Microsoft is to computers. It is a nation unto itself, with a bigger turnover than many a nation's GNP. Monsanto has been a big winner in the changing world of agriculture, with the losers being the family farm, small communities, food quality and the environment. But global reaction at the end of 1998 to Monsanto's genetically engineered products sent its share price plummeting, and forced a major restructuring as the company sought to distance itself from the controversy.

We live in a world of drug-dependency: coffee,

cigarettes, alcohol, barbiturates, cocaine and heroin. So why not make crops drug-dependent too? For instance, today when a new wheat variety is chosen, it's grown in trial plots using conventional farming methods, such as pre-emergent herbicides and synthetic fertilisers, in order to gather enough seed for commercial release. Thus no bag of new, certified seed that reaches the farmer has been grown naturally. Local agricultural events, stud sales and field days are all sponsored by chemical companies or their distributors. Everywhere you turn, someone is trying to sell you some.

Our olive grove will be balletic, moving to the music of the wind. Because we won't spray herbicide beneath the trees, there'll be a cool green mood in the grove. Groves sprayed with herbicide appear grey from a distance, and feel hot. In Spain bulldozers plough between the rows, leaving white soil to glare, whereas Italians keep their terraces grassed. No prizes for guessing which I prefer.

After fourteen years in agriculture, I've only met one farmer – a cotton and olive grower – who was actually enthusiastic about chemicals. Farmers everywhere say they'd rather not use them but are afraid not to. Many consider converting to organic or biodynamic techniques but abandon these plans at the last moment. A farmer the other day told me she was standing on the edge of change but was too afraid to take that final step. She couldn't explain the fear.

If a grower phones their local Olive Association for an information package, they will be sent instructions on using herbicides as weed control. Some olive growers are planting rye, barley or oats between their rows, poisoning them when they're tall and leaving the dead crop as a tall mulch. You could be mistaken for thinking the crop had just dried off. A tidy death.

I'm often asked, What do you do about weeds? People want a simple answer, like X kills Y, but at Elmswood we don't look for simple chemical solutions. Weeds come, weeds go. Fact of life. I've watched neighbours spraying over the years and still the same weeds return the following year. If you are obsessed with weeds, with tidiness, natural farming isn't for you, because there will always be some unwanted life on your turf. But what's worse, a few weeds or poison? When a neighbour hired a helicopter to spray thistles along the river's edge, he was doing more damage than allowing a few unwanted plants to flourish. What about the butterflies, the fish, the platypuses?

Sales representatives make a point of not telling buyers, even their retailers, about a chemical's negative side, and farmers are expected to pay for the privilege of being trained to use chemicals at courses across the state. So harmful are many chemicals that a person needs a certificate to handle them. Recently, a man spraying insecticide at a nearby vineyard collapsed. Doctors at the hospital thought it was due to the chemical he was spraying on the grapes, although he was inside an airconditioned cabin. When they read the label on the chemical drum, they saw that it advised people with a heart condition not to use it. The driver didn't know he had a heart condition. At a recent cattle meeting a beef producer said the sales rep selling him a hormone-growth promoter for his beef herd told him it was 100% safe. The beef producer didn't know that it was banned in Europe and Canada.

When we first arrived at Elmswood in 1987, I arranged to have some soil tested for chemical residues and nutrient levels. I gathered samples exactly as instructed, a little bit from here and there, and sent them off. A fortnight later the results came back and a company man insisted on visiting to explain the assessment. He said things like, 'You need sulphur here in this paddock. Nitrogen needs a lift here. But the best thing you can do is put super out over the whole lot.'

'The whole lot?'

'Yeah. With a plane. Everything likes super.'

'Why did I get these soil tests done?'

'Let's not get finicky.'

'Why does super work?'

'What do you mean?'

'Well, if you recommend I spend tens of thousands of dollars fertilising the whole farm with superphosphate, can you tell me how it actually helps the plants?'

'They like it. Helps them grow.'

'But how?'

The man shrugged.

Soil tests come in a variety of styles. A soil can have nutrients bound up in a form that's not available to the plants. Biodynamics helps release those nutrients. While farmers know that soil must contain the right nutrients if they are to grow the right plant, biodynamics goes further, insisting that the *way* the plant gets its nutrients is crucial to its wellbeing, and consequently to the wellbeing of the animals or humans that eat it.

Biodynamics was developed by philosopher Rudolf Steiner (1861–1925). While his name is principally associated with education, his theories on schooling represent only a part of his work. After studying in Vienna, he edited Goethe's scientific writings, and conducted courses in history, education, medicine, and the development of language. He turned his attention to matters agricultural just before he died, when a group of farmers asked for his help to regenerate their soils. A lecture to a hundred farmers near Wroclaw (now in Poland) marks the beginning of the biodynamic system. Steiner claimed that cosmic forces influenced the earth and that a farm must operate as a whole ecosystem. He gave farmers strict instructions on mixing and spreading a newly formulated compost, but then gave permission to fine-tune the technique.

It was Alex Podolinsky, an intense and passionate zealot, who introduced practical applications of biodynamics to

Australian conditions. I discovered biodynamics in the early eighties, while working as a researcher on a television program investigating agricultural chemicals. One afternoon I drove out to a biodynamic market garden, operated by people with physical and mental disabilities at Dural, north-west of Sydney. So appealing were the just-picked carrots, the sweet-smelling cabbages that I became one of the loyal Sydneysiders who made the weekly journey to buy the best produce around. Then the ABC's *A Big Country* screened a documentary called *A Winter's Tale*, about Alex Podolinsky. It was produced by Paul Williams, a qualified agronomist who'd been fascinated by the dramatic difference in pasture on biodynamic farms. He spent weeks filming both Alex and the biodynamic process, showing how Steiner's theories were being adjusted to Australia's broad-acre conditions. For me, and a host of others, it was a revelation. *A Big Country* received twelve thousand letters in response to the show, and Alex Podolinsky answered every single one of them. Today, Paul still gets requests from around the world for copies of his film.

At first Alex was wary of our city background and complete lack of knowledge about farming. I was forever on the defensive, trying to establish credentials. Alex made it perfectly clear he wouldn't waste time teaching us if we weren't going to be up to it. He demanded a total commitment to the improvement of our soils. After all, city farmers were forever coming and going, fly-by-nighters wasting money in the bush.

Alex doesn't suffer fools gladly, he doesn't suffer them at all. Despite his abruptness, his short temper, his impatience, he always has an interesting point of view, which he will, if you earn it, share with enthusiasm. Having at last made friends with Alex, we've been able to learn directly from him, but later generations won't be so lucky. One day, he'll have to stop travelling the country.

The biodynamic message is simple and endlessly repeated. It's about redeeming soil. Soil is the heart of every farm. It must be working, alive. Once it is dead, the farm is dead.

Our first job at Elmswood was to open up the soil in areas where crops had been grown for a century. We deep-ripped the compacted land, sowed pasture (supplies of native seed were unavailable so we planted a mixture of phalaris, rye and clover), and afterwards began spraying 500 – Steiner's mysterious, legendary biodynamic preparation. No ordinary fertiliser, it increases the biological activity in the soil, hence the name biodynamic. Instead of adding a predetermined amount of nitrogen, phosphorous or potassium, this mixture enhances the soil's colloidal action, providing an opportunity for the roots to acquire their nutrients via humus. The colloids in the soil store nutrients, so it's like humans getting vitamins from good food instead of from pills. As Alex Podolinsky says:

A naturally fed plant's needs are determined by the sun. In this situation the plant never indulges, never eats too much and all it eats is converted and slowly assimilated. In an artificial fertiliser feeding process, when the plant takes in its water supply, it has to take in soluble salts. To compensate for too much salt the plant takes in more water. Because the plant can't let go of the excess water (its high salt content would then affect it) there is less transpiration and less light intake (less natural regulation by the sun). Thus the overfed plant loses its nutritious qualities and more importantly its taste.

The 1998/99 season in the Upper Hunter was described as the best season in living memory. The grass grew and the rains came, and came and came. With so much lush feed, cattle everywhere were dying of bloat. Gasses formed in their guts and within hours they were dead, ballooning corpses, legs pointing to the heavens. But not at Elmswood. JP shifted cattle down onto pasture thick with lucerne and clovers, and people said, 'You'll move them tonight, won't you?'

'Why?'

'They'll be dead in the morning.'

But they never were. The difference was Steiner's 500.

Each year Alex Podolinsky visits to see how we're progressing. In our fifth year he plunged his fork deep into the pasture, opened out the dirt, examined the structure, and declared it good. God had spoken. I had to hide my elation.

One of the hardest lessons to learn is that you can't develop a sustainable farm by simply swapping inputs. Sustainability begins with accepting the limitations of the land. Everyone wants to believe that their land can be ever more productive, but *the land itself must define its use.*

The tide is turning, but agribusiness has long shouted down the organic/biodynamic processes. The media is happy with bigness and we're only just learning to state our case. Biodynamics will triumph for one simple reason: it works. I don't know why it works, but I don't really know why aspirin works either. And I don't have time to produce scientific papers. I do know that biodynamics and its network of farmers have found answers to intractable problems. My clipping file suggests that slowly but surely mainstream science is finding us interesting. Perhaps in the years ahead scientists will solve the mysteries of 500 and publish the results in refereed journals.

Demeter, the Greek goddess of harvest, was the inspiration for the trademark used for produce certified by the Biodynamic Research Institute (BDRI). It's not just the farm that has to be certified, it's the farmer as well, for a farmer's *commitment* is essential to biodynamics, their integrity is the greatest quality control. The BDRI sets the strictest standards in the biodynamic movement. Some of us are concerned that the word 'organic' is used too loosely, or has been entirely railroaded by corporations in much the same way as 'natural' was in the past and 'sustainability' is today.

As the global economy takes hold, our standards are being judged against those overseas, and new ones here in Australia, and there's a danger that in the name of free trade, rules will be pushed lower and lower. In 1998 the US Department of Agriculture, ever responsive to corporate requirements, wanted genetically engineered food to be included under the organic umbrella, a decision which would have had international implications. This ludicrous suggestion created such a furore, from Europe to Australia, that the US retreated.

I don't try to recruit other farmers to biodynamics. You can waste a lot of time talking to deaf ears. People question you suspiciously, aggressively, with a 'Well, convince me then' tone to their voice. If anyone is really interested, let them research biodynamics themselves. Let them read the relevant literature, visit farms and, when they want to get serious, write to Alex Podolinsky.

Many people who've converted to biodynamics speak about a defining moment when they finally accepted that what they'd been doing wasn't working any more. I shared the podium at a local field day with a fat-lamb producer who told the audience that, despite drenching, his sheep had become so weak many died. He began experimenting with biodynamics and within two years his sheep stopped getting worms and lice, and any manure on the pasture was quickly gobbled up by dung beetles. One by one, his old problems disappeared. His story, simply told, was riveting.

While I got a polite clap for my speech, he got a standing ovation. I talked theory, he told the sort of story farmers want to hear.

Farmers are giving up for a host of reasons, but in many instances the soil gave up long before the farmer. That's why Steiner was asked to help in the first place. Had the artificial fertilisers been doing a good job, there would have been no need to invent biodynamics.

Over the last twenty years Moree has become one of New South Wales' most financially successful rural shires, thanks largely to the cotton industry. The district's annual gross output is now around $1.7 billion, with half of that from farm-gate products. Yet despite this economic activity, and despite graduates from agricultural colleges flocking there to put their four-year tertiary education to the test, there's been no substantial population growth in the shire. The community still finds it difficult to attract many skilled people to the town, proving that economic growth alone isn't enough. People make communities. Thanks to television, cinema, magazines and advertisements, few now choose to live in what they perceive as isolated towns, despite the economic opportunities. It's a conflict between two cultures: the excitement of the urban and the satisfaction of the rural. Culture is really the deciding factor for most people who want to live in the country, and the rural culture that is promoted as most desirable is that which isn't very far from the city. Unfortunately for Moree, it's eight hours from Sydney. It's closer to Brisbane, and has been begging for decades for a direct rail link to that city. So Moree, with an economy nudging $2 billion, can't create the critical cultural mass that draws the crowds. Culture needs more than money.

Scone, on the other hand, is only four hours from Sydney, or under three if you drive like Phillip. It's within that perimeter of desirable rural areas, largely because it's close enough for locals to use Sydney for their principal amusements. Entertainment has, after all, become a spectator event rather than a participatory one. And as long as people choose to venture 280 kilometres for a 'nice night's entertainment', as Dame Edna puts it, Scone will be the poorer culturally. Over the years there's a been a huge push from the council, the Local Business Centre, and any number of groups to promote Scone as a tourist destination. Early critics insisted the shire's priority should be providing basic services to its ratepayers. Now it appears that tourism is deemed foremost in every rural centre's economic hopes. No matter how hopeless the prospect, committees pretend that their dull town is a theme park, they yearn for fame and its financial benefits. All over Australia, local communities are staring at the ceiling trying to come up with ideas to lure the tourist dollar, and most are doomed to stay staring at the ceiling forever. Why not be honest? Instead of having silly signs at the edge of villages saying, WE'RE A TIDY TOWN, they should simply say, WE WANT YOUR DOLLAR.

From its domestic origins, valued for protecting crops from mice infestations, the cat, reluctantly domesticated, became one of Egypt's gods. Now, sadly, it's a feral creature around the world and a problem in our district. The only cat we have is a 3000-year-old bronze version in the sitting room. Phillip shoots real ones on sight. On sentimental occasions I try to convince myself that cats have a legitimate place somewhere in Australia, but I'm still not sure where. Phillip jokes it's in the casserole dish. Needless to say, Rory loves cats.

In *Feral Future* (Viking, 1999) Tim Low talks about exotic species taking over our landscape and concludes, after three hundred and sixteen pages of powerful argument, that 'biological pollution' is a greater threat to the world than either greenhouse warming or industrial pollution.

Our latest feral example is a fish.

'There're carp in the river,' says JP sadly as we head off to the back cattle yards for a happy day cutting testicles from young bull calves.

'What carp?'

'The carp that are going to wreck the river. I've seen them.'

'Has anyone else seen them?'

'Everyone.'

'I haven't.'

'They're there.'

Then why isn't it front-page news in the *Scone Advocate*? Or have we become so accustomed to ferals that we're resigned to them? Carp was, I thought, the one problem we didn't have. They were something that happened in the Murray–Darling basin. Bottom feeders, they muddy rivers, destroying habitats, and thereby help kill off native fish. And now they've found their way to the Isis and the Pages.

Feeling guilty that I haven't been observing the river more closely, I decide that, from now on, whenever I turn on a pump and sit on the bank while Rory splashes around, I will search the ripples for evidence of the aliens. We'll walk along sections of river we've rarely visited, just looking for carp. But I'm not sure I can tell one fish from the other.

'You'd know a carp, Patrice,' Phillip says when I admit my ignorance. 'They go,' and he pouts his lips and does a fish impersonation. 'And you'd know them from the Edo screens in the living room. Don't tell me you haven't noticed them?' Not another art lesson coming up, I think, one should never admit to ignorance. 'Of course,' I say unconvincingly, trying to remember the images painted by a long-dead Japanese.

Months pass, with not a carp in sight.

Halfway through 1998, when we add up the monthly rainfall, we realise it is going to be the wettest year we've known. The river has become a real river, really flowing, and we feel it has acquired a sort of permanence. The depth of greenery along the banks is so thick I am seeing new colours. Rory wants nothing to do with our rectangular swimming pool, she wants the river to be her *Wind in the Willows*. But instead of Mole, Badger, Rat and Mr Toad, she has Kangaroo, Cow, Duck, Eel and Snake.

But still no carp.

What was JP talking about?

Each day as we drive to school, we stop on the bridge for a moment and do a stocktake: three moorhens, two lapwings, an egret, occasionally a spoonbill, at high flow a pair of pelicans. And always ducks of various types, often with ducklings. But what delights Rory most are eels and catfish. There's usually one huge catfish down below the bridge, in a shaft of morning light. 'Catfish is there,' Rory announces happily as if that makes it safe to drive on. She slumps contentedly back in her seat, sure that all will be well with the river while she's at school.

Then comes confirmation of JP's report. A dairy farmer tells me that carp are making a bloody mess around his place. And the very next morning Rory rushes into the kitchen to raise the alarm. 'Carp! Mum, there's carp below the bridge and the catfish's pool is all muddied.' Oh no.

Down we go. Phillip was right, I do recognise a carp when I see it. They're doing Phillip impersonations with their mouths. The disease has spread after all. And our little catfish, our barometer below the bridge, gone?

Carp is the most abundant freshwater fish in the world, and now in Australia. It's also the most widely eaten fish in the world, and yet here its image as the imperialist of our waterways has kept it off our dinner plates. Carp have been with us for over a hundred years, released in ornamental government ponds and the impressive Centennial Park in Sydney for decorative purposes. It wasn't until the 1960s that alarm bells began to ring. Carp had escaped an experimental aquatic farm in Victoria and begun breeding in the Murray River. By the 1970s they could be found in most waterways in eastern Australia.

Although the image of carp is unequivocally negative – that greedy fish ruining the waterways for our native breeds – I'm not sure they're as bad as I first thought. For a start, they're herbivorous and they don't eat juvenile fish. So our pet catfish – and let's face it, I really can't tell one catfish from another – could well have simply moved downstream, where it's illuminated by the morning sun as it always has been, except we aren't noticing. Furthermore, if our river becomes full of them, I should start serving fish for dinner more often. And when the Pages River stops flowing, as it will during the next drought, the carp will disappear back downstream and it could be years before we see them again. After all, our abundant waterways during 1998 and 1999 have been the perfect breeding ground for all fish, not just carp.

If carp had already been in the Pages River when we arrived in 1987, we'd view this latest feral activity with less concern. Like we do weeds. Acceptance is part of the equation in controlling anything unwanted. But here is something new. Pushing at the boundaries of the unwanted. Representing more work, more understanding, more consideration in the scheme of things on our farm.

'I'm not gardening any more,' I tell Anna, my comrade in spades and forks who has a genius for gardening. Her suburban plot is testament to her Italian/Spanish/French heritage and her way with plants. Where I struggle with every seed and bulb, she seems to conjure growth with an elegant gesture. 'I simply don't have time. We're planting an olive grove instead.'

'An olive grove! That's a *big* garden, Patrice!'

Our little house garden is a corridor between the colossal demands of farm and homestead. When either overwhelm, the garden beckons, inviting me into its soothing, dishevelled nooks – casual, jumbled, but beautiful nevertheless. A place to potter, to sit; a halfway house with the sky for the ceiling.

Once it was a simple place. Then an environmentalist told me, unaware how miserable his words would make me, that gardens would soon be a thing of the past. 'The garden is the source of so much unwanted plant material that will eventually go wild.' And he's right, in the sense that every garden plant is a potential weed. But I will not give up the right to grow roses and salvias and lavender. Am I simply putting my aesthetics ahead of my ethics? Yes.

Walking up a distant hill, I once discovered, in full bloom, a circle of thousands of purple and white iris. They looked as though they'd been formally planted, but by whom? I searched around for clues. Had there been a hut here? Later I learnt that, yes, there'd been a humpy on the hill, built by one of the men helping Terry with the rabbits. In due course the iris will spread far and wide – another beautiful problem.

I like seeing evening primrose by the side of a track, or even the few surviving prickly pear (Rory loves the fruit), and even the curse of briar brings the benefit of rosehips. So much of what I love was brought to the wilderness by good-hearted pioneers. The CSIRO lists as weeds one hundred plants originally grown as foods.

The previous owner of Elmswood told how she'd tried to grow only the plants that were fashionable at the turn of the last century, thus keeping the garden in harmony with the house. She marched me around, obviously proud of her achievement, but I could see no evidence of a garden plan at all. No hedgerows, no arboretum to show off, just a lot of grass-covered iris beds with tired-looking shrubs and trees in need of radical pruning. There was no grandeur in a handful of scrawny ten-year-old eucalypts, three *Celtis occidentalis* and a deodar cedar. I was not acquiring a garden at, or even distantly approaching, its evolutionary peak.

I didn't have a plan either, but I certainly had fantasies. I wanted the place to be a lush, chaotic shambles. The whole area needed to be thickened up and massively planted with evergreens. Soon I was wasting money at nurseries and popping things in the ground willy-nilly, with little thought to design, soil requirements or watering needs. I was a victim of all the romanticism of my childhood, of my mother's love of Wordsworth and Keats, and I would soon be a victim of droughts, frosts, rabbits, hares and cockatoos. The Vita Sackville-West books I'd read were irrelevant here.

Others could waste money on extensive irrigation networks and full-time gardeners, I had to find another, more appropriate idea.

On a visit to Western Australia I saw a garden that brought design and dryness together. Planted beneath native eucalypts were clumps of lavender and rosemary, the verticality of the trunks creating a cathedral-like enclosure in the middle of nowhere. I like gardens to make me look up. And adding to the religious feeling was a font, left symbolically dry. I walked along paths of rammed earth between hardy plants that brushed my ankles and thighs. The overwhelming mood was of Australia and dryness, with soothing shades of grey, blue and purple.

I couldn't prevent fountains with water popping up in our garden because Phillip collects them. Realising the artefacts couldn't remain piled up next to the shed forever, he invited his mate Frank or, Fountain Frank as he calls him, up to Elmswood.

Frank's truck rattled up the drive filled with strange things. He'd scrounged copper cylinders 3 metres in diameter, and welded brass dolphins around the outside for overflow spouts to be used as pond edges. There was a copper Moorish cap, quite useless, which we'd bought; a weathercock; a glorious bird bath – a metre-wide copper ball cut in half and moulded onto a stone pedestal. We filled this oddity with water and lilies and fish, but the copper promptly cooked them, then the mosquitoes made it their haven, so we emptied it and filled it with plants. Now it's another *thing*, decorating an already well-decorated garden.

By the time Frank left, we had a French terracotta fountain outside the kitchen, a bronze one with dancing maiden amongst the fernery, and another virgin holding a water container on her shoulder in front of the pencil pines. We'd already inherited a lily pond with a three-tier stone fountain at the front of the homestead. True, all had small, recirculating pumps and were parsimonious with water, but I couldn't approve of the symbolism.

Sometimes garden statues and pots get buried in foliage, not to be seen for years, only to be remembered when I clip back the ficus or ivy. I know there are two French urns smothered by sedum somewhere below the steps. I've been trying to think of another place to put them for years, but there they remain hidden, a cool spot for dogs, a refuge for lizards, a favourite for snakes.

Decades ago the garden was fenced in with a strange geometric arrangement of wires and wood. For some peculiar reason, the style changed at every strainer: four wires in one section, then all barb, then white-painted wood or post-and-rail. It could have been used as a fencing display. Gradually we pulled it down. Now the unfenced, undefended garden flows out from the house and becomes the farm. The lawn blurs into the lucerne paddock – it's made some farming practices difficult. When a drought reaches a critical point and every tuft of lucerne is precious, we string electric fencing tape – a white, 2-centimetre strand with wires through it to conduct the electricity – around the garden. Bulls either jump it or brush it aside to drink from the lily pond, munch the lemon balm and chives, and tear at the delicate flowering pear. But it's a small price to pay for a fenceless garden. And I half enjoy the challenge of trying to teach animals of very little brain that what's theirs is theirs, and what's mine is mine.

Visiting the art-supply shop on Sydney's Oxford Street one day, I try out the brushes on my arm and cheek. Twisting and turning them, I sense their invisible marks on my skin and eventually buy a selection of delicate brushes. On translucent rice paper I draw up plans for an elegant parterre, to be planted on a low, level piece of ground where, with great excitement, we'd demolished the tennis court. What a useless addition that was. 'You pulled down a tennis court!' people would say in astonishment. Yep. Couldn't wait to get rid of it. What did they think this was? The Garden of the Finzi-Continis? There'll be no white skirts worn here. We take our eye off the ball.

Once the space is cleared, so many possibilities become evident. We seriously consider a mud-brick shack, before proposing an arboretum, a formal rose garden, then a walled garden to hold a collection of rare vegetables. But so far we've done nothing. This is the last big bare space and I'm savouring it. Dreaming of possibilities is more fun and a lot less work. And I have to be sensible sometimes, we can't manage what we already have.

Desperate for a new vegetable garden, my old one now too shaded by fast-growing trees, I ask Keith to put up a fence of chook wire around a patch of lawn. It's simple and crude, and I love it. The utility of this site, its reference to sustenance charms me. We didn't dig up any grass. By simply spreading out lucerne hay and dumping loads of our homemade compost on top, it is instantly ready to plant and soon is bursting with vegetables -- there's always something there to eat. It makes sense to have a messy vegie patch, where lettuce, arugula, chicory and herbs can self-seed, and planting three broccoli every few weeks is better than a neat row that ripens all at once. We had so much silver beet one year I was feeding it to the chooks. Their egg yolks turned a deeper yellow, my cakes and quiches so bright they looked artificial.

Some garden designers talk about the strength and serenity of the straight line and dismiss curved garden beds. They're also snooty about using rocks as borders. But curves are natural at our place, not just in the garden, but across the land -- the rising hills, twisting rivers, the wind curving through the trees. A line of sight is straight, providing an axis, but we have no straight plantings, no clipped hedges. I see the argument for classic lines and, when they're well executed, appreciate their form, approve of their formality, but they are harsh impositions, so for me they don't work here.

Some parts of the olive grove are full of rocks. We're forever removing them so we can take the tractor down the rows without wrecking the slasher. Mostly we lift the rocks by hand, but some are so huge we need help from the back hoe. Once they're heaved onto the back of a truck, Phillip moves them to a part of the lawn where, he assures me, he'll convert them into his latest installation. It's not a wall or garden edge, but a circle of rock, 15 metres wide and rising. At present, though, it's a snake pit.

'What a shame that spiky old thing is there,' visitors say, confronting a spectacular example of *Gleditsia triacanthos* growing in the lower garden. Many find it ugly and it's certainly dangerous to approach. Its 12-centimetre spikes, resembling those of an echidna, could blind you if you weren't careful, but I wouldn't move it for the world. The last garden tree to flower in spring, it was in 1988 the inspiration for a major planting of hundreds along the road to the cattle yards. At the time it was praised by the Forestry Commission as a fodder tree (something cattle can eat during drought), though lately they've damned it as a noxious weed. But I admire the way it defends itself and I love the drama of its seasonal changes. Flowering brings the deafening hum of bees. For months it's bright green, then bright yellow. And autumn reveals clusters of thick pods that dangle from the branches like bats.

I've just had an idea. An underground storage area for olive oil where the tennis court was!

In the summer of 1995, before olives had entered our lives, we were in Berlin. The Wall was down, Christo was wrapping the Reichstag, and the city was jubilant. While Phillip was broadcasting, Rory and I caught the train to the botanic gardens. The roses were blooming, but to reach them we had to wade through willowing grasses, some 2 metres high. One morning a young boy came hurtling through on a ride-on mower and cut pathways around the roses. Further along, amidst unlabelled trees, a team of elderly men and women resembling Breughel's peasantry were scything a meadow, raking grass into rows for collection in wooden wheelbarrows. Finally they built haystacks that were pure Monet.

'Let's do that, Mum!'

I looked around for the film crew. Could this really be happening? In one of the most modern of modern cities? I investigated and found that the botanic gardens were very proud of their meadows and this was standard practice.

The paradox continued. Not one median strip in Berlin was mown. Not one front lawn – in contrast to the farmland, which presented an almost military precision, together with all those nice new tractors in nice newly restored barns.

Back home and inspired, we create, for a few short weeks, something I've always wanted. The perfect house-meets-garden-meets-farm-meets-national-park look, and all because we don't cut the lawn. ('Lawn' is probably a big word for the mowed weeds around the house.) What a spring it's been this year. A season when the thistles aren't so bad because the rain has come too late to stimulate a mass germination. Instead the paddocks are full of useful things like clovers and grass. There's a carpet of bees across the lawn, attracted by the Haifa white clover which once introduced proliferates anywhere water goes. Up it's come, spreading its spotted leaves. The straight, light-green shoots of rye have poked through it, together with the less desirable, broader-leaved barley grass. Fine when young, it irritates once the barley matures and the spikes crawl all over you. I have to remember not to wear wool, otherwise they're up your sleeve in no time. Lucerne, wild oats, yellow weed, and myriad other herbaceous plants proliferate along with daffodils, jonquils and bluebells, and soon the grass is up to our knees.

One afternoon I march around the garden, Phillip following me on the tractor with the slasher attached. In minutes we have paths, and for the next two months we mow nothing else. A fifteen-minute job once a week, and again it's perfect. The rest is pure joy, like having someone else's garden where there's no compulsion to work. Not once do I think that a plant needs to be moved, pulled out, pruned, tied back, fed with manure or watered. All is enchantment and I am in love. I actually sit on all those logs we've put under trees, or on the seats and chairs we've strategically positioned and never used. There is more time in the day. Kids discover a secret garden, play hide-and-seek and jungle games in the tall grass.

But the rule of opposites eventually prevails. What is wet becomes dry, what's up comes down, and so with the garden. The rains stop, the winds blow and all the flowering grasses brown off. Now Phillip is alarmed by the prospect of a bushfire. 'We'll be incinerated.'

Phillip insists on cutting the grass, but I triumph. Instead of just mowing it, I have it turned into hay and our meadow is neatly stacked in the shed. It has been a time of magic in the life of our farm and garden.

I suspect that I don't really want a garden at all. I want to live in a wilderness.

The noisy slurping of olive oil, making it spread across the palate and explode over the tastebuds, is officially called aspiration. I'd read about it, then saw and heard someone do it. The hissing intake followed by expectoration into a cup, or, worse, a cup stuffed with a paper napkin, isn't the most enjoyable experience. But it doesn't take long before I can be seen at grand provedores in Melbourne and Sydney pulling the same grotesque facial expressions and spitting. In fact I show off, proving that I can be the noisiest taster in the room. Look, if you can't be heard you're not doing it properly. I start fooling around with friends, until it dawns on me that I'd better get serious. Oil tasting will be as important to us as wine tasting is to the vignerons.

From my first mouthfuls of high-quality olive oil I know I want to make a bright-green pungent oil, the kind that burns the back of the throat, makes pesto magnificent, and looks fresh on the plate. My preference is influenced by my love of Tuscany and by my ignorance of southern Italy where a golden, milder oil is preferred. The flavour of Tuscan oil has evolved as a consequence of meteorological necessity, because the fruit has to be picked before the frost attacks.

Most Australian provedores tell us that consumers don't like oils that are too raw, powerful, cutting. They like their olive oil bland, golden and boring. While you can occasionally find good flavour in a sweeter oil, I know I don't want to produce it. If it were wine and the market demanded chardonnay, I'd still be determined to produce a cabernet.

I attend my first serious tasting in Florence, where set out before us are oils in coloured glasses – appearance isn't supposed to count. We're told to codify subtle differences in our memory, relating them to other tastes or experiences – rancidity reminds me of the whoof of fat you get up the nose when you open a packet of potato chips, making you suspect the quality of the oil used to fry them – at the same time learning a standardised vocabulary for characteristics, both good and bad. Let's face it, there's nothing harder than describing a flavour, as the pretentious prose of wine writers remind us.

Despite more than two millennia of olive oil consumption, it was only in 1994 that the International Olive Oil Council first accredited tasting panels, attempting to standardise organoleptic assessments. Previously, virgin oils were categorised only by their chemical composition. The key factor in chemical composition is the free fatty acid component. If there's less than 1% it can be called extra-virgin; between 1% and 2%, virgin; between 2% and 3.3%, ordinary virgin; and more than 3.3%, lampante, the latter being so hideous that it has to be reprocessed before it can be sold as 'pure' olive oil. It should be avoided at all costs.

But just as oils ain't oils, virgin isn't necessarily virginal. Once an extra-virgin oil has undergone chemical analysis, it's supposed to be assessed by a panel before it can claim the title, for even an oil with a low acidity can still taste awful. It must also be free of defects in smell or taste. The official list of defects includes: fusty, musty, winy, vinegary, acid, sour, muddy, metallic, rancid, and others. If any of the above are found, its extra-virginity is denied.

Rancidity caused by oxidation is the most common defect and is the easiest to detect. A metallic taste eventu-ates if the oil comes in contact with unwanted metals during processing and isn't unlike the sensation you get when you accidentally crunch on a bit of alfoil. Winy, vine-gary, acid or sour qualities are all painfully obvious and are caused by an excess of acetic acid, ethyl acetate and ethanol. Muddy sediment in an oil smells of the earth and generally derives from storage problems. Musty oils recall a stuffy cupboard, a mixed stench of humidity and fungus. And a fusty quality, for me probably the most difficult qual-ity to discern, comes from fermentation.

Once the defects are exposed, you can move on to the

positive attributes, such as fruity, bitter, pungent. These are the basics. Just as wine writers keep stretching the verbal envelope, oil 'experts' keep adding descriptors: flat, smooth, apple, almond, burnt, rough, greasy, soapy.

Australia's first organoleptic school was held at Adelaide's Roseworthy College in 1996 and was conducted by Luciano Di Giovacchino, who'd trained European tasting panels. He was invited back the following year to teach the first Australian Sensory Assessment Panel. I don't see olive oil tasting becoming as popular an event as wine tasting. Oil is first and foremost a fat, and while a good oil doesn't leave an unpleasant taste on the palate, a bad one does. Nor do olive oils improve with age. So there's no reason to buy a special bottle and store it reverently in a cellar, to be produced for a special occasion. To store olive oil is to ruin it. The best oil is the freshest.

The most important thing the consumer can do is read the label to establish the date of pressing. If that happened overseas more than twelve months ago, forget it. If it's Australian and one year old and there's no other choice, take the risk. The chances are it's been stored well and at least it hasn't had to cross the equator. It's best to buy small bottles often. I've made some expensive blunders by not being vigilant. Once, having spent a small fortune on some imported oils, justifying the expense as market research, I returned to Elmswood and, with appropriate ritual, opened a bottle to enjoy the fragrance. Only to gag – the oil was off. Not merely rancid, but putrid. After twenty minutes with an Italian dictionary, I'd translated the blurb on the bottle to discover that the oil, priced at $80 a litre, was three years old. Useless for salad dressing. Overpriced for saddle dressing.

It can't get any busier. I lie in bed, surprised that the first month of winter has passed and I never saw the early white jonquils under the elm. Before breakfast, Rory and I rug up to stroll in the cold garden, boots cracking iced puddles and leaving footprints in frosted grass. 'Can we pretend it's snow, Mum?' Sure. Spiderwebs, delineated with dew, connect the garden with their fragile threads. Peace. Beauty. Then Rory starts jumping around singing the Monty Python song about a lumberjack working all day, putting on women's clothes and hanging out in bars.

We all feel different things.

In February, at the height of summer when the kids have to go back to school, I'll dream about winter. I'll have to, to be convinced the heat will end, that relief is imminent, even when it isn't. That the flies will go away. That I'll want to cook again. Okay, so in summer we can pick baskets of apricots, plums and peaches from the orchard, but being in a 40-degree kitchen making batches of everything isn't all fun. When it's 38 degrees we comfort ourselves by saying, 'It's not so hot today.'

Winter is the time to enjoy the fruits of our summer labour: puddings and scones with the jams we make, hearty stews with the beef we raise. Winter isn't a slow time. We work twice as much, inspired by the freshness in the air. At night Phillip and I stay up till all hours by huge fires.

Wherever we go, Phillip collects wood. His pile, or rather piles, around the house are surging sculptures. When they get too unsightly or too comfortable for unwanted beasts, I beg him to stop. Just as some people talk about the food they make ('I think this needs more lemon, the chicken's a little underdone'), Phillip invariably comments on the way his wood burns: 'That piece is from the ironbark down near the crossing where the dozer was last week. Look at it, it's been burning for an hour. This box tree smells different to the one near the chicken coop.' He watches fires as they work their artistry throughout the night, handling each piece of wood as if it deserves a place in his art collection. Some pieces he hates to burn and returns to the pile. He's been admiring them for years.

We have so much wood, but there should have been more. The previous owner called the timber cutters before we moved in and cut down a whole valley of trees. It was like coming upon a war zone – shock, horror, disbelief at the sight before us. What a mess! What a waste! Huge trees felled, severed, murdered; the valuable timber of the trunk removed, the rest left to rot. We've been burning the limbs ever since, but it would have been better to have had the trees alive, flowering, seeding. When the local timber miller tells us there's almost no old ironbark left in the district, I tell him we've millions of young trees out the back. 'Look after them, luv,' he says, 'they'll be worth more than beef soon.'

In another valley the trees that weren't cut down were poisoned. Tall-standing corpses still clearly show the axe wounds into which the venom was poured. And trees are still being poisoned today. Driving over Crawney Mountain, an hour north, we come upon a vertical hillside covered in dying trees, the brown leaves hanging on determinedly. No legislation stops this wanton killing.

Two teachers, Stuart and Heather, have just completed their impressive mud-brick home north of Scone. They didn't incorporate a fireplace. 'In the long run, Patrice, wood fires aren't sustainable,' says Stuart. A house with no fires? Another thing to feel guilty about. What an unimaginable future!

Barrie, the dozer man, is a tree lover. When he's not being paid to push them over, he examines ancient fallen trees, identifying the timber and collecting rare woods. 'A tree can be dead for decades, but the wood inside is still good,' he tells me. He's salvaged enough fine timber for his son to build a house. I like following him around Elmswood while he climbs over fallen logs, rattling off their Latin names.

Bosnians chopped down municipal trees to stay alive in winter during their war. We have enough dead trees to warm a thousand houses, yet we've planted thousands more, in an act of penance.

There have been many light dustings of frost this winter of 1997 but nothing too bad. Winter is a time to refuel, before the cycle of life begins again. Hibernating lizards and snakes have the right idea, as do deciduous trees. Olives too need winter to activate their internal clock, to set fruit in the spring. But the cold they need is qualified; the temperature mustn't descend too steeply, nor the cold last too long.

This winter the ground is especially hard. The temperature is plummeting. My hands ache and I can't unfold my fingers. Working outside before ten o'clock is misery. Some cattle need hand-feeding; JP is putting out silage bales for all the weaners and heifers, and soon we'll probably have to hand-feed some cows. Sparse autumn rains have left the paddocks without much feed, there'll be poor nutrition for the calving season. Everywhere we go people are murmuring about the smell of drought. 'Is it dry out your way?' they ask, knowing the answer, wanting to share some bad news.

Drought is only ever six weeks away. My first destroyed all my preconceived ideas about developing land. Evidence of hard effort and investment simply disappeared. Could it be happening again? Could it? Although we associate drought with summer, winter exposes its shocking intentions. A dry winter feels considerably colder than a rainy one. The air cuts. Every deep breath slices your lungs.

I can read the mercury in the thermometer on the patio, but the discolouration of shrubs, the sad decline of leaves tells us more of what we're experiencing. Summer vegetables collapse first. Basil and tomatoes convert to sludge once the temperature hits zero, and the lawn dusts white. But we expect that. Usually by the end of April I'm cutting up the green tomatoes with the red, to make sauces more piquant, and I've made more than a few jars of relish so generally I'm happy to see the vegies reach the end of their season. We've had enough tomato bruschetta with pesto. And the appetite for beans is finite. Once they've been dug up, there's room to plant peas and English spinach.

We enjoy the stillness winter provides, the excuse to stay indoors reading, talking, playing with Rory. Knowing that we don't have to be an appreciative audience for the olives, applauding every shoot, we rest together with the grove. As the cows give birth and calmly tend their offspring, the olive trees, I hope, will be standing strongly erect, happy and quiet.

Some frosts fall like bombs – you can almost hear the plants scream as the water freezes inside them. Other frosts arrive gently, stay most of the morning and thaw delicately. There's always one humdinger every season, when pipes freeze in the night and don't thaw until lunchtime. I try to sense its arrival, have a bath in the evening and fill the saucepans with water. The plant that best indicates the humdinger is the white osteospermum halfway down the garden, planted beside a thick clump of flax, not far from a crab apple. It will hang on, flowering and green, until the humdinger gets it.

Elmswood is colder than almost anywhere else within a 20-kilometre radius. I know this because we alone can't grow jacaranda and lemon-scented gums. June, July and August are officially winter, although August is usually springlike here. Winds arrive from all directions and warm afternoons anticipate the excitement of the new season, but I don't plant tender annuals like cucumbers until October. Together with September, August is ambiguous. I put winter and spring together and for eight weeks have a season I call winning.

But we don't win on 27 August 1997. I awake to find the pipes frozen. I open the blinds to see an endless sheet of frost. This could mean minus 10 or 12 degrees. With Rory still asleep, I rug up and rush downstairs. Crushing iced grass, I stare at the osteospermum. It's burnt brown. I know what this means.

Now I run towards the grove and find the trees snap-frozen. Not slightly wilted, not tipped by frost, but completely, totally, unequivocally frozen. Most have been in the ground just three months, some only six weeks – the tallest would be a metre high, the stems half the width of my little finger.

And they're dead.

Staggering down the rows, breathing in and out becomes painfully hard. The muscles in my chest tear as I heave across the paddock. I discover olive tree after olive tree wilted, yellowed, shrivelled. Am I screaming aloud? Frost? Only frost? Olives are meant to be hardy. And this is the winning season.

It's an irony that a fall of snow wouldn't have mattered. Snow is a different, less destructive form of cold.

Finally I stop and scan the grove. Yes, it is all dead. The white coat of frost, so beautiful, is a murderer.

Sinking to the ground, I weep.

JP is in the new grove on the hill, above the shearing shed and, thank heavens, above the frost line. I manage to stop crying before he reaches me. But I think he's going to burst into tears too when he sees the devastation.

'Olives aren't meant to be stressful. They're the tree of peace. They're not giving me peace,' he says bitterly as we walk up and down the rows, hoping to find a section that's survived. What we do find, from time to time, is a single, solitary tree in perfect condition. One here, one there. Why? They're like the lucky ones who walk away from a fatal smash.

We phone Di and Ray up the road. Their trees have been in the ground for nine months, did they get the humdinger? I'm ashamed to admit it, but as I dial their number I'm hoping their trees are as devastated as ours. I'm in the mood to share. Di says she hasn't been to the bottom of her grove as yet and will ring me back. I wait by the phone. Twenty minutes later I hear her hysterical voice. 'Patrice, I think they're all dead!'

JP and I drive straight over. Yes, they're dead all right. We return home hoping for a miracle. The day is warm, the frost is gone, it feels like spring; the almond and plums, planted on higher ground, are in full blossom. Everything *is* going to be all right. But the dead trees look even deader.

I phone Phillip in Sydney with the bad news. I'm always phoning Phillip with bad news, like 'The neighbour's just run over your dog.' Or 'A fox has eaten your white peacock.' His response is invariably the same: a long silence, and then, 'Don't worry.'

Seeking more understanding, I phone Andrew Burgess at Olives Australia, where we bought the trees, and have a long, heartfelt whinge. Instead of cheering me up with accounts of other tragedies, he tells me of people who've planted thousands of trees and haven't lost one. I feel worse. So I try to blame him: 'If only your trees hadn't been so small, perhaps they wouldn't have been so affected.' But small trees were my choice, the hole you dig doesn't have to be so big.

While we consider the implications and I ring the experts, we stop all planting. Amongst the string of explanations, I'm accused of not watering enough and watering too much. Frost can make the tips brown off but the trees can handle it. A frost is harder when the ground is drier. I keep thinking our problem can't be just the frost.

We've been obsessed about over-watering, believing that olives hate wet feet. Now the frosts keep coming and we keep turning the irrigators on. And every day I return to the devastated grove, looking for signs of regrowth that some experts promise, the little shoots I'm told will appear just above ground. But when?

I go to Brisbane for a meeting on beef grading and arrange to call into Olives Australia at Grantham with some of my dead trees. There are rumours that the soil fungus phytophthora is killing trees. Could this be a factor? Antonio Berenger, who owns a huge olive nursery in Córdoba, Spain, happens to be visiting Grantham when I arrive with my dead samples. I'd lifted two trees out of the ground, roots and all, and wrapped them in plastic. Antonio immediately points to a split just above the soil line, a swelling, a slight tear of the bark. 'Frost!' he declares emphatically. And then adds, 'It may not have been so bad if you'd watered more.' Okay, okay. So it's *all* my fault. 'Below the tear mark it's still green,' he says, scratching at the bark, 'and spring is here after all. They will reshoot.'

I phone Phillip with this news. There's the usual pause before he says, 'So don't worry.'

Frost damage isn't as bad as phytophthora. A bit like a diagnosis of cancer versus dropping dead. They might shoot. They might not.

Back home from Brisbane I want to stay in bed all day. It's hopeless. Olives don't like it here. They don't like us. They're not easy trees after all. They're just another farming folly. And I've wasted a year of my life and a lot of money. I go out and buy butter.

Phillip keeps the fires burning, I make steamed puddings with loads of saturated fat, pour fresh cream over the top, put my feet up and try to feel happy.

Ann, a fellow beef producer, phones for a gossip. 'We went to Jayne's *formal* fortieth birthday party on Saturday. The men had to change places at the end of each course and I got stuck next to old Smithy for desert. I always respected him, but he's really just an old boring fart.' Thus begins a dialogue on how men can slowly build a reputation in the bush only to lose it at a birthday party. I like Ann, she never discusses anything serious like politics, religion or dead olive trees. She's just what I need.

There are more slight frosts and word spreads about our disaster. Olive growers leave sympathetic messages on the answer machine: 'Don't let a freak frost dishearten you.' 'What doesn't kill you makes you stronger.' A week later the soil test results are faxed. No phytophthora. Now I know that the frost is guilty, guilty, guilty. And if it's killed once, we know it will kill again.

Way behind with the cattle work, we shift attention to fat and muscle scores, loading one truck of steers for export, another for Sydney butchers. I bank cheques the following week. Cattle breeding has never been so easy. Hundreds of cows have calved in the hills. The calves, Hereford and Angus, are playing together, scampering around their mothers. They're so cute. I *love* cattle breeding.

Then it rains. A little. JP rushes over, exultant. 'The olive trees have reshot. They're not dead, Patrice. They're alive!' Down we go and, yes, they're shooting. I forget my miseries, just like I forgot the pains of childbirth when I first held Rory. A tiny pinhead of green has formed at the base of every tree. And every snail, bird and insect will want to eat it. How are we going to protect them? Each day they'll push out a little further. As we clear the weeds away, I wonder how anything so small and fragile can give such hope.

So let's finish planting! JP reploughs lightly and carefully over the rows we'd marked out, leaving dramatic stripes of black amongst the green. I'm watching. It looks good.

The next morning I throw open the windows and spring smells delicious. The threat of drought has passed.

The vision is pure Van Gogh. I feel like I'm in Provence. The only thing missing are the vermilion poppies, but then out prances Rory wearing a poppy-coloured cardigan. I could easily spot her miles away. Yes, this is a happy place to be.

Weeds begin flowering too. Now the black stripes of soil are yellow-edged, you'd think it was a crop. Yellow weed, or turnip weed, is a brassica – a common spring intrusion around here. It arrived years before us, and despite annual slashings to stop it seeding shows no sign of surrender. It will look perfect between the olives and already has the grove abuzz with bees. A local beekeeper tells me there's little nectar in the yellow-weed flowers, but they're a stimulant that gets the bees in a frenzy for work. Friends arrive to help plant but are so fearful of being stung they retreat to the kitchen and cook. Which is fine by me.

For a few days JP and I just keep planting. At night, tired but optimistic, I plump the cushions on the sofa and return the many phone messages.

Beware! Country women talk about their visitors. A week wouldn't pass without some gossip about a poor weekend guest who thought onions grew on trees, was frightened by chooks, fell off a pony. I add my story about asking a city friend to pick some broccoli from the vegetable garden. She came back with the entire crop, twenty flowers, thinking she was doing me a favour. And there was the bright August morning when Rory's school friends picked *all* the strawberry flowers. I'm opposed to corporal punishment but favoured capital punishment that day.

I almost forgot the organic retailer who paid a visit with his dog, a Jack Russell, that leaped out of the car and chased my beloved chooks all over the garden. 'Oh isn't my little doggie cute, chasing all those little chickies.' The look of heaven on its face was not reflected on mine. Insane with rage, I caught the dog, thrust it into the arms of the owner and yelled at him to lock it in the car. Such was their stress that the chooks didn't lay for three days.

Then there was the morning I awoke to the braying of donkeys, only to discover the entire herd milling beneath the bedroom window. Rory's friends, staying overnight had got up early and, deciding the donkeys would enjoy greener grass, had ushered them into the garden where they showed a marked appetite for roses, especially Lamarque, which had been particularly hard to grow.

Very few city visitors are at ease in rural life. Most arrive physically and mentally exhausted, and having planned a short visit will leave in the same sorry state. To enjoy the essence of a farm you can't be passive. You have to reach out and embrace it. It demands engagement. Elmswood isn't simply a house in the country, though that's what most people perceive it to be, it's a place of endless work and activity, with the homestead its headquarters. There's always too much going on. Phone calls to make, cattle weights to be faxed, prices to be negotiated, bee stings to swab, cockatoos to shoo. It's good when visitors get into the feeling of things and don't expect to be entertained. Unless of course they've come merely to sleep and then I can justifiably ignore them. Even if visitors leave refreshed, I'm often exhausted.

Food writer Maggie Beer believes people should learn restaurant etiquette. Cancel early, and cancel rather than come in a bad mood. When you're there, don't talk too loudly. In other words, remember you're in a public place and behave yourself. Similar suggestions should apply to farm visitors.

It's late on Sunday and David is pegging out the site for our new barn. It will overlook part of our struggling olive grove. I stand where the verandah will be and wonder if the shoots of the frost-damaged trees, invisible from here, will have the strength to fight the odds and survive. Will the barn forever remind us of our failures? Edna and Rory are collecting insects. Phillip is reading down by the river. I walk back to the kitchen to prepare for dinner and wait for David's assistant Paul to arrive with his crane. A massive hoist, permanently clamped on the back of his truck, is to be used over the next few weeks to lift the poles and frames into place.

Having worked with Paul on many building sites, David admires his talent and reliability. But I'm worried about him. Last week in Sydney, Paul forgot to lower the crane correctly when he drove away from a job and promptly snagged the electricity wires at a busy intersection, thereby wiping out the power in four suburbs and causing melt-downs in innumerable electric motors and computers. Businesses were disrupted and claims for damages will surely follow.

Eventually Paul's truck heaves up our narrow driveway, crane down, and out he climbs with his wife and two small daughters. You can see the weight of the world on his shoulders. Over dinner we talk about the accident, all of us accepting that in life you're forever skating on thin ice, that the cold waters of disaster, random and mysterious, await us all. Six days ago, had someone told Paul what the future held, he wouldn't have believed them. Perhaps working on the barn will calm him down. By the end of the night we're laughing. In the morning another five men will arrive and the building of the barn will begin.

Soon there's a sculpture of massive ironbark poles. We've planted a Stonehenge of dead trees. Fifty-six all up, 2 metres down in the ground, some rising 10 metres into the air. These are real trees, individual trees with scraps of bark dangling; we're not talking the anonymity of dressed timber here. David has spent hours deciding where each pole should go, imagining how knots and curves will appear in the finished building. This pole for the front, that for the back. This high, that low.

I want the barn-in-progress to be left as it is. The way Michelangelo left sculptures forever emerging from rough-hewn blocks of Carrara marble. In the twilight the barn looks eerie and magnificent. Can't we build another one somewhere else?

As the weeks pass, a wooden flesh begins to cover the bare bones of the poles. David and the team bolt the bearers into place and lay sheets of plywood to make it safer to walk and work. But it is still necessary to move cautiously from bearer to bearer. David has remarkable balance. He dances around, strolls the timbers like a tightrope-walker, forwards and backwards, without seeming to look at his feet.

Finally we're ready for the raising of the roof. We've argued for months whether it should be new-style Colorbond, forever green, or traditional shiny galvo. I'm for Colorbond, arguing for subtlety and less reflection, but David and Phillip, sticklers for tradition, win the day and the roof becomes a beacon. One that visually connects to the homestead's galvo roof, preserved by layer after layer of silver paint applied to keep the rust at bay over the hundred-odd years of its life. Now the barn joins it and together they glow like a rural parody of the Opera House. It should be on the map for aviators, to guide them to the Scone airport.

Yesterday we could stand in the barn, look up and see the stars, as if we'd built an observatory for a giant telescope. The poles lifted your thoughts and your head. Now, with a roof, the building becomes human, practical and contained, and we start thinking different thoughts.

While David is in Sydney for a few weeks, Phillip decides that the verandah, which was to wrap around the building, shouldn't. He wants the space inside, not outside. So over my protests he tells David, on his return, to move the walls out, thus doubling the interior space. David obliges. The walls are made of ironbark planks that have been curing in stacks in the hayshed for months. Having been sliced from trees of differing sizes, each plank has a different patination and width, so the walls will have a rough, gutsy feel to them. In the olden days, thin slats were placed between axed slabs to keep out draughts and vermin. But David has a better idea. Using a round saw, he makes a slit in the middle of each slab and inserts a strip of brown-painted galvanised steel, forming a kind of tongue and groove, thus joining the slabs forever. If there's to be more shrinkage, all you'll see is a hint of brown paint.

Sawdust piles up around the building site as each slab is cut into shape, and wafting on the wind is the smell of sap. Day by day, slab by slab, the walls go up, the interior darkens, a secret is being made. Window frames and doorways are on order, but already the poles have framed the grove, the river, and the hill in Pennyroyal Paddock. The framed landscape changes by the hour and we're reluctant to break it up with small panes of glass, so we decide to buy a vast piece of laminated safety glass, 1.8 metres high and 3.8 metres wide, which will be a nightmare to install. David makes inquiries and discovers another complication: the only piece of glass available is in Adelaide.

Insulation bats are pressed beneath the galvo, and a pine lining nailed precisely into place forms a cathedral ceiling. The pine is bright and lightens the interior a little. We choose flooded gum for the floorboards, buying seconds to save money. The boards are dramatically knotted, but I like that.

Laying tongue and groove around fifty-six poles is the most tedious of tasks, but David gives a beaming smile and says, 'Building the barn has been magnificently flowing.' With a quiet ceremony, we nail a little brass plaque commemorating David and Paul's contribution to this immense project.

Now Phillip can spend the next ten years filling it, and our upstairs bedroom will be free for a bed.

A few winters ago we rented a lovingly restored stone farmhouse with sky-blue shutters near Orange, in northern

Provence. Beyond the house was a goat farm, where two women made cylinders of fresh goat cheese for the local markets. During winter they'd stopped making cheese to concentrate on the birth of the kids. Each morning, Rory ran across the fields through the cold mist to the barn, where a kid-cubby had been made out of straw and heated with red lights for the newly-borns. Rory was allowed to nurse these day-old floppies and oversee their feeding. In the afternoons, hearing the goat bells in the hills, Rory made believe she was Heidi meeting Peter the goatherd up the mountain. Out she'd race, climbing a terraced hillside of derelict olive trees. Between patches of snow the ground was covered with spindly thyme and lavender, and the scent would waft down to meet me as I watched her disappearing in the direction of the bells. She'd pat the little nanny-goats and watch them trying to climb the trees, resting their front legs on an olive branch to tear at the leaves.

I asked the cheese maker why she didn't resurrect the grove. She shrugged. Her goats pruned them, that was good enough. She was more interested in the herbs, as they were what made her cheese so fragrant, so special. Meanwhile the trees were slowly dying, covered with scale and olive knot. I yearned to tackle the grove myself with a pruning saw. The local French don't want to salvage the past, so they leave their stone cottages and build modern bungalows. Most of the love poured into old things in Provence comes from Parisians or foreigners. Our cheese maker was French but grew up in Switzerland. The owners of our rented cottage were Australian. One neighbour was from Texas, another from England.

Now, as I kneel planting at Elmswood, Rory stands back and says, 'We'll need goats to prune the olive trees, Mum. And I'll milk them before school and make cheese.' I don't say no to her goats. I love her dreams and suggestions, but I've just learnt that foxes take about 10% of the olive crop in South Australian groves and JP has discovered we've dozens of feral goats in the back paddocks. And goats eat olives.

By mid-October you can feel the heavy heat of approaching summer. The flies have hatched and constellations coat the back of our shirts as JP and I change the rhythm of our work, planting just a few trees every day. The thousandth tree is about to go in the ground, but it's hard to celebrate as I look back at rows of dead stems. Yet planting becomes therapeutic as, finally, life exceeds death. After a few days we realise we've planted more new trees than the six hundred or so crushed by the frost. We're balancing the score.

We've failed to meet the planting schedule, so set new deadlines. We have to complete this section before JP can walk amongst groves of hundred-year-old trees in Spain and Italy.

The year before, in October of '96, I was in Europe with

twenty-four other crusaders on a tour conducted by Olives Australia. After a meeting at the International Olive Oil Council headquarters in Madrid, we ventured out across Spain to Jaén, Córdoba, Seville, before being seduced by Tuscany and Umbria.

Then, I'd travelled without feeling the discomfiture of a dying grove. Now, after a year of unfolding disasters, I yearn to return to those old groves to gaze at contorted trees that have survived so much, so long. But I must settle for the vicarious pleasure of JP's first trip overseas. It will bring all the reference books to life and allow him to gather together the threads of history, culture and tradition. This for a man who rarely leaves the Hunter Valley. He pretends to be casual about it, but it's impossible not to see his excitement and anxiety. As we work, there's banter about immigration procedures, the temptations of duty-free shopping, and whether jetlag is fact or fiction. I tell him how Norman Gunston used to get buslag when travelling between Wollongong and Sydney.

I plant the tree I've been holding in my hands, imagining it strong and tall, and see myself older and calmer, wandering through the grove with Rory's daughter. I see her climb the tree, hang from its sturdy branches, and this connects me to all the other olive trees I've planted or will plant, trees connecting Gundy to Europe, the present to the past. And this tree with its frail roots I'm about to place in the earth has its roots in the olive trees that grew long before the Old Testament was written.

The Egyptians revered the olive. Hercules' staff became an olive tree. The first Olympic torch was a burning olive branch, and the first Olympians wore wreaths of olive leaves. The Bible's two testaments talk of olives a hundred and forty times, with the white dove bringing an olive branch to Noah's Ark, signalling that the Great Flood was, at last, in retreat. There's the story of Christ at the Mount of Olives and the tradition that he died on a cross of olivewood. Has any other fruit been burdened with as much legend and responsibility? Yes, one. The apple, that cursed Catholic girls like me with Original Sin.

The water on my skin isn't ladylike perspiration. I am raining. Though I used to pay for saunas in Sydney, I can't enjoy this. JP and I work together in the heat, in silent competition, taking pride in not giving up first, not complaining. It is madness, but won't always be like this. There'll come a time when we'll be working beneath, in and around the olive trees, not *on* them like now, where we provide the shade for them. 'When can I climb an olive tree?' Rory asks. Soon.

Swallows swoop from the shearing shed, nattering on the wing. There's at least a dozen nests along the eves or across the beams. Their Jackson Pollock droppings decorate the wooden poles and floorboards. Visitors are drawn to this old wood-and-galvo building, the smell of lanoline, stencils hanging from nails, an antique wooden bale press. The shed is rough with use. When we came here we sheared two thousand sheep. Now the generator starts up with a shudder when JP and his mates shear the few we have left. We'll always have to have a small flock to keep the building alive. Shearing sheds need sheep.

It's Wednesday and it's been 40 degrees every day for over a week. And now the pump at the rapidly shrinking river is playing up. We've ordered new parts but they won't arrive for another week. JP has arranged for his son Matthew to help while he's away. A plumber, Matthew will still be going to work each day, but will be around in the late afternoons if I need a hand.

We fear for our baby olive shoots. We need every drop of water for the trees. Finally we quit planting and start lugging water in drums and buckets. Then I suggest JP has a quiet two days, otherwise he'll want to sleep on the trip.

For the first time Phillip is unsure about coming up to the farm at the weekend. His mother, Sylvia, is very ill and he's been making repeated trips to her bedside in Melbourne. After *Late Night Live*, he phones the hospital and is told she's stable and comfortable. So he leaves the ABC studios in Ultimo and makes the long regular drive to Elmswood, arriving at 2.30am and sneaking, very loudly, into bed.

JP arrives early the following morning to discuss what needs to be done while he's away. I make tea and the three of us sit out on the patio, where Phillip regales JP with stories of terrible plane journeys, near crashes, and the time his Qantas plane was struck twice by lightning as it flew over the Vatican. He grins at JP, who doesn't grin back. Keep quiet, Phillip. JP's had a haircut, and as he says goodbye he looks so quintessentially Australian, I suggest we send his photograph to Qantas for their next ad campaign.

We don't leave the house because Phillip wants to be near the phone in case the hospital rings. His daughter Meaghan calls with reassuring news. I make stock for risotto and plan our formal Friday night meal at the long dining table, for which Rory dresses up, festooning herself with her grandmother's jewellery. Usually this is funny, but with Sylvia so ill it's deeply poignant.

Saturday, Rory and I get stuck into the vegetable garden early, but there's no water. We go up to the tanks on the hill and they're both completely empty. With the pump out of action we'd moved cattle to a paddock with dam water so they wouldn't access troughs, so I know cattle haven't damaged a float, causing one to overflow. But we drive around anyway, checking every trough, and then across the paddocks where I know the pipes are buried. Rory is on the look-out for a bright green bog amongst the brown grass. But there's nothing. It doesn't make sense. The water has to have gone somewhere.

By now JP will be at Mascot, nervously, excitedly climbing aboard a jumbo, and Phillip is asleep. Wasting water is the only issue that sends Phillip into paroxysms of rage. If anyone is caught wasting it at the kitchen sink with surplus rinsing, he'll immediately deliver a lecture. He instructs visitors to take thirty-second showers. So when both a 30 000-gallon tank and a 10 000-gallon tank are mysteriously empty, you can understand why I'm not anxious to tell him about it.

'Rory, let's go up to Gundy and get the Saturday papers,' I say. I might even read them in the car.

'Can I have a treat, Mum?'

'Two,' I say. Anything to keep the peace this morning. She beams at the prospect of an icy-pole and a lollipop.

When I get back to the homestead Phillip is sitting at the table, drinking the first of many cups of tea. Meaghan has just phoned to say that Sylvia has had a bad night and Meaghan will call back as soon as she's talked to the doctor. In the hallway Phillip has restacked his boxes of work, ready to be loaded back into the car. We sit around, only pretending to read the papers.

Like me, Phillip is an only child. Like me, only his mother survives. Rory and I said our goodbyes to Sylvia weeks ago, when her strength was greater and she still wanted to talk. Today, Phillip wants to be with her alone. There's too much to say, too much to feel, and he looks so very, very tired. He can't wait any longer for the phone call and heads for the car. Standing out in the wind we wave goodbye.

I need something, anything, to make the day speed up, to take my mind to a place that doesn't hurt. So I think about JP on the jumbo and hope he's got the window seat he was counting on. Then it's back into the truck to look for that elusive leak. Driving up the road, I turn off and explore the contour of the hill where we'll eventually plant more olives. It's been deep-ripped and some pipes have already been laid. But I don't go far. Suddenly, I'm bogged to the axles. Days ago JP was dragging the Agrowplow across the paddock to eliminate a germinating weed, and he must have dislodged a joiner. Now I'm in a quagmire, and revving the truck is futile. All I've achieved is a precarious tilt. Rory, sitting next to me, excited by the noise, shakes her feet above the dashboard in delight.

'Where are your shoes?'

'I don't know, Mum.'

Where is St Christopher when you need him? Feeling like the patron saint of travel lugging baby Jesus, I step into the mud with a heavy five-year-old on my back and immediately lose a boot to the suction of the mud. Slowly, wearily, I plod back to the house, keeping Rory's bare feet from sharp gravel and dry thistles. She thinks it's great.

I can't bear to go outside again, and spend the rest of the day sitting around in a daze, waiting for bad news to complete a life's story. Circling my mind are the words from near the end of *The Great Gatsby*: 'tomorrow we will run faster, stretch out our arms further . . . And one fine morning –'

Yes. One fine morning. Is Sylvia's fine morning about to dawn? Phillip calls from the domestic airport at Mascot to say he's just missed a plane but has arranged to catch an international flight to Melbourne. So Phillip follows JP in climbing on a jumbo. He phones again from the taxi on his way from Tullamarine to the hospital. I try and stay up, to run faster, to stretch out my arms further, but eventually fall asleep.

And Phillip never made it to the hospital in time.

I drop Rory off at a nearby farm to spend the day with her best friend and leave Phillip clearing rocks in the olive grove. Packing my knapsack with an apple, sultanas, a bottle of tank water and Ian McEwan's *Enduring Love*, I set out on an expedition to the very back of the property. I can't ride a horse out there, it's too mountainous and I'm too nervous, although I keep telling myself that one day I will ride over every inch of the place. For now, however, I hike.

Usually I'd drive to the first gully, about 2 kilometres away, but today I start at the homestead, cross the river flats and start trudging up Dam Paddock, looking down on a stretch of water alive with yabbies, tortoises and wild ducks. The paddock is a treeless hill that usually annoys me with its stubborn refusal to respond to our efforts to improve it by slashing, tree planting and light grazing. But I'm oblivious to its disappointments today. Sadness is making me see *everything* differently.

I used to think Elmswood was overcleared, that too many trees had been sacrificed, but there are differing opinions on how heavily timbered the hills around here were before white settlement. Certainly some parts do quickly self-seed when we remove stock for long periods, but other hillsides, where I long for regrowth, seem determined to remain barren.

I *take* time here, walking. I'm not wasting it. Walking is thinking. I'm feeling the inside of thoughts.

Gates have been left open since JP moved the cattle to a distant paddock, so I tramp on, not needing to wrench wire rings from rusty latches, or drag their heavy frames, or put back on their hinges those that have been dislodged by amorous bulls. I cross the plateau once used as an airstrip, now the cause of ethical concern. In the past we let our neighbours use the strip for spreading superphosphate, the planes roaring between the gum trees, just clearing the barbed-wired fences, but as the creeks and rivers filled with the consequential algae we started saying no. Sorry. Not any more.

Descending into a deep gully, I follow the creek bed, lined with whispering she-oaks for hundreds of metres, to a point where four gullies converge, creating a dark rock pool. Fringed by native clematis and used by cattle and kangaroos in the evenings, this is one of my secret places. I dump my bag, pull off my boots, strip naked and slide into the sharp water, and stay there, flapping around until the heat of the hike is gone and I start to chill. As the air dries me in the warm dappled light, it's time for Ian McEwan. I've been reading him for decades, ever since his first collection of short stories. It's become a family joke. 'Reading your boyfriend again, I see,' Phillip will observe when he sees a McEwan book lying around, which is often because I always read books I like more than once. And when he finds me reading someone else, he'll say, 'Christ, Ian will be upset.'

McEwan is as familiar as this favourite place of mine. Here, I escape my dramas in McEwan's. I join him in England in the traumas and confusions of his characters. McEwan writes wonderfully ominously of landscape, finding threat and tragedy everywhere. His story and language move in and around me, but I'm in no way confused, for my landscape, like his, has sorrows and menace all its own.

A water goanna drops from a she-oak into the water and I close the book in surprise. Dressing and repacking the knapsack, I continue along the creek.

The water has almost stopped flowing over the rocks, which means I can lunge across them without getting wet boots. The sun, considerately, is hiding behind thick white clouds. With the glare subdued, I heave upwards. There's a heavy-set wallaroo labouring up the adjacent hill and I remember he's near one of the beehives I put out months ago. There'll be little honey flow, the weather has been so harsh, so dry. I detour anyway and observe, from a distance, the bees zooming in and out of their painted white box, busy as usual. In the next hour I see no other animals. No cattle, no kangaroos and no wallabies. They're all sensibly asleep in the shade somewhere. And no snakes either. Even the birds seem eerily quiet. It's like a stage set after the actors have gone. I, the solitary member of the audience, am the only movement.

I'm far away from the soft, domesticated hills around the homestead. I'm into the wilds, into a different climate, heading for a summit which, in hard winters, is dusted in snow. The temperature is dropping, the trees huge, the views epic.

Climbing effortlessly, I arrive at the top before I'm prepared for it and lean against a boulder twice my height. Below me is Elmswood. Beyond, in the middle distance, Glenbawn Dam harnesses the Hunter River; beside it, the Segenhoe Valley is full of posh horse studs. On the horizon the vapour from the chimneys at the Bayswater power station lingers motionless, like exclamation marks. I see with some concern the continuing encroachment of the surrounding coal mines, devouring vineyards and cattle country alike. Sydney is four hours further on.

This place. This exact place is where I want to be. Not beside or near these hills, but on and in them, enveloped by all their secrets and sorrows. For they have survived their injuries, and over time healed themselves. I want to learn their lessons.

Nine hundred metres below and 10 kilometres away, I

can just see the suggestion of our first olive planting. Their future is far from guaranteed. Leaning against my rock, I close my eyes. Pushing grief, pulling joy.

When I left the homestead four hours ago, I felt depressed and exhausted by too much death, Phillip's mother, hundreds of newly planted trees, even the death of many naïve dreams. Now, far from being tired from the long climb to the peak, I feel renewed. The contrary tugs of life throw up so many considerations. Yet here and now I find an equanimity, a place far more difficult to locate as I get older. The clouds move and the vermilion tint in the air dusts the leaves and shadows. I remain still for a long, long time.

Venturing down the steep path, lightly, easily, the tendrils of home reaching up to me, I imagine the future of our olive grove, seeing it ancient and grey, undemanding, its foundation firm in the landscape.

Seeking refuge in landscape is what hundreds of others, are doing across Australia, this very moment. Almost a century ago, my reclusive grandfather Morton Colechin regularly walked in the wilderness beyond Melbourne. Some of my favourite photos show him at campsites, tent pegged, billy boiling, his children, including my mother, and occasionally his wife by his side. Serious, purposeful walking was a popular pastime at the turn of the last century, particularly for men with their sons. Those philosophical walkers, together with our poets and painters, helped us understand the bush.

The appreciation of nature was becoming formalised in Australia by 1914, when Myles Dunphy set out his objectives in his journals, eventually published as *Selected Writings* (Ballagirin, 1986). He wanted 'wholesome recreation – full appreciation of the senses, cultivation of the faculty of observation, powers of endurance and self-reliance – regard for welfare and preservation of natural beauties that lie about'. He organised his mates into the Mountain Trails Club and began to take a professional approach to his hobby, establishing the best routes, swags, shoes, clothing, tent styles, equipment – developing, as we'd say today, world's best practice. And in the process he became a leading conservationist.

Though a full-time architect, Myles wrote thousands of words on natural history for newspapers and journals. Had he extracted a small section of his notes and reworked them into a literary narrative, like Thoreau did in the previous century, Dunphy would perhaps be more famous today. While Thoreau spent his time alone describing nature and life around a small area of Concord, Massachusetts, Dunphy, together with a team of walkers, mapped his way across vast tracts of New South Wales. In *Walden*, Thoreau romanticised a humanised, tamed landscape, whereas Dunphy celebrated a wider, wilder world. Thoreau saw splendour in the woodcutter as well as in the wood, while Dunphy derided those 'puny men with axes', blaming them for the destruction of the landscape. (Would Thoreau be pleased to know that much of the countryside he knew and loved has been reclaimed by forest, with old roads abandoned, houses and barns collapsed?)

Taking a step at a time, Dunphy and his son Milo began gathering support for national parks in New South Wales. Oddly, it was the Labor Party that joined in his campaigns for the bush, wanting to save those uninhabited places between farmland and accepting Dunphy's view that 'the world was not made for any one particular generation alone'.

'Whether we like it or not,' wrote Dunphy, 'we hold our land in trust for our successors.'

In 1934 he challenged people to 'measure correctly the needs of the future'. I'm trying to do that almost seventy years later. We may not be able to predict the future, but we can appreciate the past and influence 'he evolution of our landscape.

It's November 1997 and I sense the approach of another drought. This time I recognise the symptoms. The cracks in the black basalt are widening like the fissures in an earthquake, eucalypts are defensively shedding their leaves, rocks appear to be growing in the paddocks, kangaroos are descending from the hills and will soon be occupying the garden. Snakes too are slithering on the patio, and we see their tails disappearing into Phillip's wood stacks.

And once again the river is hardly flowing. At lunchtime I phone a few mates upstream to find out who is sucking it dry. Clearly what's left of the river is being squirted across lucerne paddocks. All that's left for us is algal sludge and dank pools of water. With JP still in Europe, I'll need to check the dams every couple of days. Most are low, having never properly filled since the last drought. The cattle look fine, but can slip quickly.

I enjoy reading the meteorological reports in the broadsheets, just as I once enjoyed announcing the weather at the end of the SBS news. As the names of cities rolled up the screen I'd read from my auto cue, 'Fine today in Tokyo. More cloud in Seoul.' Now I want to imagine what JP's experiencing. In Madrid, where it's raining. Or Rome, where it's also raining. Poor JP, it's been miserable across Europe for weeks. Mud-slides have wiped out towns, an earthquake at Assisi has left thousands homeless and damaged the Giottos in the basilica. I remember gazing at the frescos early one morning when the choir was rehearsing, and racing back in the afternoon to glimpse them in the failing light. JP's Assisi will be very different.

I retrace my Europe in memory. While the Spanish may be the biggest producers of olive oil, it's the Italians who've created its seductive associations with virginity. It's in Italy where the oil has become most ritualistic, where you learn to taste oil, cook with oil and feel its promise.

It was in Italy that I met Chris Butler, a fit, prematurely

white-haired Australian who, like me, comes from Adelaide, has worked as a journalist, and is notoriously sharp of tongue. Needless to say, I liked him instantly. I also liked the fact that he'd done what others simply talk of doing. Thirteen years earlier he'd packed up and moved to Tuscany determined to write plays, imagining a future of poetry, passion and pasta. But he arrived when the countryside and the ancient olive groves were being devastated by frost. Locals hired him to salvage what they could, and soon he was up and down the terraced hillsides pruning with a small chainsaw.

Next, he negotiated accommodation in return for maintaining a grove of fifteen hundred trees, and promptly set up his own consultancy. Within a couple of years he was well known throughout the Italian industry and had met just about every Australian interested in olives. His advice and comments were always brutal. 'Anyone with a grove under fifty thousand trees is a hobby farmer,' he told me.

It was in-your-face Chris who'd organised the Italian leg of our Olives Australia research tour. For ten days he herded us through chambers of commerce and arranged encounters with eccentric organisations like the International Movement for Olive Oil Culture (MICO). We met scientists, growers, distributors; visited dilapidated castles, historic groves, and different kinds of processing plants boasting new ways of pressing fruit.

On a typical day, he'd gallop us over the Ponte Vecchio for a lesson in the rigours of tasting with the *grande parmigiano* Marco Mugelli, who conducted a session translated by Chris, with all the theatricality you'd expect at La Scala. Then we'd meet Guiseppi Grappolini, President of MICO, who'd orate on the need to 'give a clear and dignified identity to a unique and wholly natural food straining under the weight of misconception and commercial manipulation'. (Today MICO has almost folded and Chris is no longer their International Director.)

The days were so jam-packed with factories, facts and figures that going to bed early would have been sensible. But heck, we were in Tuscany. On our last night, when we were exhausted and overstimulated with olive information, Robin Love, who works in Hollywood as an agent for movie crews but who is talking of coming back to Australia to plant olives in the Hunter Valley, produced a restaurant review from the *New York Times* and suggested we go. So a group of us meandered off into the night looking for a restaurant called Cibrèo, an unpretentious, not too noisy, white tableclothed eatery. It was that meal – fresh whole porcini, polenta, autumn vegetables, and loads of olive oil – more than any other on the trip, that seemed to capture the reason why we were planting olives in the first place. Olive oil is a great enhancer. When used properly, it can turn a good meal into a masterpiece. It's like finding the right adjective for a sentence. I knew then I'd found the right adjective.

JP got his window seat. On every leg of the trip, he sat with his nose pressed to the perspex, ignoring the offers of magazines, the availability of in-flight movies, and looked down in wonderment at the world below. When his fellow travellers complained about the tedium of the terminals, JP found fascination in every one of them. Few travellers will have travelled with the intensity, enthusiasm and curiosity of JP Gilbert from Gundy. But JP, being JP, took his time in telling me, or anyone else for that matter, about the trip when he returned. He is infuriatingly laconic.

'Well? How did it go?' I asked when he lumbered up the back stairs.

'What?'

'The trip?'

'Oh that.' He grinned.

As expected, Italy caught his imagination. How could it not, with Chris Butler in the Tuscan hills indoctrinating him with passionate reason.

Then it began. First a trickle of words, impressions, then a flood of repressed excitement and photographs. Out came a confusion of memories: Chris Butler showing him pruning techniques; the Swiss guards standing at the doors of the Vatican; the small, nut-brown men of Spain; olive trees flourishing in the harshest places; the peaks of the Swiss Alps passing beneath the wings of the Boeing; the Pope conducting Mass; olive fruit being crushed by new stone mills, exactly the same as those built hundreds of years ago; the tiny little cups of coffee in Rome.

These were not stories he'd be able to tell at the local pub, where fellow drinkers had not shared his excitement at the news of his trip. He'd been troubled by the lack of interest, the resentment, the jealousy. But in the weeks ahead, he never stopped talking to his family and to us about what he'd seen, smelt and felt. He told Phillip that his life had been changed forever, and from the moment he got back he dreamed about going again somewhere, anywhere, anytime.

Despite all the excitement of the trip, it didn't take long for JP to acknowledge the encroaching drought. There was no time to lose for cattle, for olives, for water. We got stuck straight back into it – planting, weeding and mulching in 40-degree heat and cutting winds.

The next day was as hot as hell. I passed JP in the morning as I took Rory to the school bus. Lifting fingers from steering wheels we gave each other the standard rural salute. I assumed he was going to check the water tanks and that we'd meet up soon afterwards. Back at the homestead I did a few chores, checked a few trees, but there was no sign of him. Looking out across the hills, I couldn't spot his Toyota. What was up? The next few hours are a blank. For JP and for all of us. His wife Margaret eventually phoned: he'd turned up at home totally disoriented, with a complete loss of short-term memory that lasted for weeks.

It had happened once to Phillip, so I recognised the symptoms immediately.

Later we would joke about it. About JP forgetting all the adventures he'd had in Europe, about the entire trip simply disappearing. But the day it happened and in the days ahead, it was terrifying.

Poor JP. It was the ultimate cruelty, the world's most enthusiastic traveller robbed of his travels. It was as if Casanova had lost all memory of his seductions, Captain Cook of his voyages. There was nothing physically wrong with JP, at least nothing that doctors and tests could find, so we put it down to the heat, and mercifully his memory fully returned. But the fright it gave us made us realise how much we all cared for him.

Even without bouts of amnesia we were all over-stressed. What we needed was some perestroika.

JP's son Matthew had always been part of Elmswood. We first knew him as a skinny little kid in primary school, then as a lanky youth in a plumbing apprenticeship forever being borrowed by JP for farm jobs. Matthew never complained. He loved farming, and as time passed he realised he loved it a lot more than plumbing. He started to talk about getting a job on the land. My instinct was to offer him a job immediately, but Phillip was concerned about the problems arising from a son working for a father. But with the pressure of work mounting and the drought deepening, I started tentative discussions, first with JP who was immensely enthusiastic, and then with Matthew whose response was immediate. He could move into the cottage beside the homestead, help with the cattle and learn everything about olives.

'Matthew, when is the earliest you can start?'

'Two weeks.'

'Brilliant.'

Plant on. We must plant on. It's a chore watering hundreds of trees in pots, and they're getting root-bound. We must get them into the ground. On weekends Phillip and I get up at four-thirty, have tea and toast, start planting at five, before the sun scorches us. By nine, we're in the pool recovering.

Fellow olive grower Harvey, who's heard about our dramas with dying trees, turns up unexpectedly for the guided tour. First we stand on a hill for an overview.

'There's green grass near your trees!' he says with alarm.

'Yes, that's right. We've been watering. And it's brown between the rows because the rye grass has died off, flopped over and looks as if we've laid a natural-fibre mat,' I say proudly. I think it looks wonderful. Occasionally, nature does exactly what you want.

But Harvey isn't appreciative. 'I want the grass around my trees to be brown.'

In other words, he wants it poisoned. Why bother coming? I think. This is a biodynamic farm!

JP is feeding the last precious bales of hay to cattle that are losing condition by the hour. I phone Digby and Helen, biodynamic farmers at Ebor, about four hours north-east, in the hope they can accept some on agistment.

'Come up and have a look,' says Digby.

Being certified A-grade with the Biodynamic Research Institute means we can't send cattle to just any old farm for a holiday. Digby and Helen's farm would be perfect. It's cool and mountainous, creeks are flowing, dams are brimming, and the grass is waist-high. Nestled in a nook, looking like a gingerbread cottage, is a stone house they've built themselves. It's a remarkable, romantic building, the last thing you'd expect to see in the landscape. But then Digby is full of surprises. He shows us a little hydroelectric gadget spinning in a creek that provides enough power for lighting, cooking and heating. Best of all, he shows us the paddocks available for agistment. And their cattle are just like ours. They'll get on fine.

The reason our cattle and his, and those of other biodynamic farmers in the region, are alike is because we're all in a sphere of influence created by an improbable eccentric from Tasmania, Peter Chilcott. Chilcott is an enormous man. Rory is in awe of his tummy, the biggest she's ever seen. Peter will lean on a fence and moo to distant cattle so convincingly, so fluently, that they come lumbering towards him, convinced he's a bull or a cow or calf. Such is his depth of knowledge. And what he knows is this: cattle's bones should be flat. This is the Flat Bone Method, the biggest secret in the beef business. When bones are flat, or better still concave, the meat fibre is finer and denser, and therefore more tender. Round bones indicate tough meat.

I was first introduced to this method at the annual general meeting of the Biodynamic Agricultural Association of Australia, where Digby and distant neighbours Albert and Gilbert Hancock were displaying the jawbone of a recently killed steer. It was passed around and handled in a way reminiscent of Hamlet stroking Yorick's skull, with a mixture of fascination and reverence. We all got to rub our fingers up and down the bone, marvelling at its flatness.

Chilcott will arrive at a farm, haul his stomach over the fence, talk to the cattle, rate them from tough to juicy, and signify their merits with coloured ear tags. And, as we discovered, it works.

We learnt how to test the jawbone and sometimes the rib cage as well. There were doubting Thomases in abundance, but those of us who followed Chilcott's principles were soon having spectacular results. A guarantee of tenderness is a valuable asset for a beef producer. One of the problems with forming marketing coalitions of any type is the discrepancy between each other's product. Being different in soil, water and feed, each farm inevitably produces a different – albeit only slightly different – product. And modern marketing is predicated on consistency. By using Chilcott's tenderness scoring, we could aspire to a guaranteed quality, regardless of who raised the cattle.

And there's another aspect to the Chilcott theory that, as a feminist, I find deeply attractive. In the macho world of beef production, where men are men and women unwelcome, there's a lot of bull about the bull. The bull is first and foremost, and the cow comes a bad third. Men strut around cattle yards discussing the size of testicles as though the bull's virility were their own. I remember at one cattle sale hearing a beef producer say of a pen of cows, 'There's nothing in there that will give me a hard-on.'

Chilcott is like Germaine Greer. He sees things very differently. He bases his breeding on the feminine flat-boned cow. 'It's all female-related, Patrice,' he tells me. Cows should be soft of face, maternal of instinct. Bulls are over-rated, cows under-appreciated. I remember him looking at our cows and saying, 'It's smell, you know. Like with humans.' Chilcott, a newly married man, took a deep breath.

We truck over a hundred cows to Digby and Helen's.

This drought, I tell myself, isn't going to be as insufferable as the last. The only problem is we can't agist the olive trees as well.

I call 1993 the Year of My First Drought. After three parched months, JP and I drove to a crisis meeting in a community hall about an hour north. By now we'd been hand-feeding cattle for weeks and our hay supplies had dwindled to a few thousand bales. One of the problems with hand-feeding is that the cattle congregate, turning a paddock to dust. It was spring and already the days were hot, further evaporating the muddy, slimy dams. JP would load the back of our trucks with the precious hay and I'd load Rory, then one year old, along with tapes of *Winnie the Pooh* and *Play School*, and a rudimentary picnic to try and make an adventure of it. But the experience remained deeply depressing.

The whole district crowded into the local hall for the meeting that night, farmers cracking bleak jokes about how we were all stuffed. The beef officer from the Department of Agriculture talked about the levels of nutrition you can get from hay of various qualities, and silage if you were lucky enough to have it, and from molasses if you could afford to buy it. At the time, cattle across the state were being 'fed' by desperate producers with cottonseed meal, a waste product of the drug-addicted cotton industry: this caused another residue scandal that temporarily slammed the doors on Australian exports.

Old-timers who'd endured a dozen droughts, including the monster in the eighties, were blunt with their warnings: you can hand-feed, suffer the cost and get exhausted; you can dump all your calves on the market and kiss this year's income goodbye; you can agist the cattle if you can find somewhere; or you can do nothing and be damned. Every option led to catastrophe.

'If you decide to sell,' the Department of Agriculture bloke said, 'this is what you should do. Old cows aren't worth keeping. Neither are heifers. Cows around three and four years are the best ones to keep, they've already proven themselves. Take their calves off *now*, sell them, and hand-feed the cows if you can.'

It was a gloomy drive home.

'JP, we're going to have to sell the back paddock herd.'

'Yep.'

These were the oldest cows on the place; despite being part Brahman and supposedly genetically designed for dry times, their bodies had lost so much condition it was pitiful. They looked like the Brahmans I'd seen eating plastic bags on the streets of New Delhi. I knew how JP must have been feeling. He'd been hand-feeding that group the longest and was very attached to them.

Beef producers hate selling calves prior to weaning when

they can be worth $400 or more later on. When I phoned the stock and station agent the next morning he offered $20 each for our six-week-old calves. They were taken off their mothers the next day and sent to an abattoir that, having been closed for many months, had reopened to handle the flood of starving cattle. Our veal was exported to Europe where it fetched a hefty price. With a heavy heart I phoned our regular abattoir to book in the cows. Everyone else at the crisis meeting had phoned before me and I found our cattle had to join a long queue. They couldn't help us for another two weeks, which meant we'd have to waste hay to keep the cattle alive, further deepening the financial crisis. Even getting a truck would prove difficult. The whole district, almost the entire state, was losing its herds and it would take us years to recover.

To add injury to insult, the truck that finally arrived wrecked the cattle yards. It wasn't our usual carrier, and the young driver backed into the loading ramp with such force he shattered the cement and splintered half the wooden uprights. I wanted to send *him* to the abattoir.

In between I spent hours on the phone trying to sell some veal at a decent price. I wasn't going to sell another calf for $20 knowing it would be served up in a restaurant in Munich for $20 per schnitzel. I started to get some interest from restaurants with a nose for a bargain, but then I struck another problem.

Local butchers were flat out cutting up animals sent in

by local producers to be loaded into farm freezers. This way, they'd get something out of the disaster, enough meat for the family for the next two years. So once again I had to join a queue. Finally our veal was being cut up in between jobs by butcher friends like Michael and Murray Towler, who were working eighteen-hour days. And I began delivering to some famous name chefs.

I organised some Sydney butchers as well, and spent long days driving around the suburbs delivering cuts of biodynamic, milk-fed veal – at a third of the price they were used to paying, if they could get it at all. This was a once-in-a-lifetime special because we were desperate.

Most restaurants were pleased to help out, especially after hearing my sorry tales of the drought. But arriving early one morning at a posh Italian restaurant in the eastern suburbs, expecting a warm welcome from the head chef, I was confronted by his mother instead. In her seventies and as arrogant as any prima donna, she took advantage of her son's absence to give me hell in full volume, viperlike *la lingua italiana*, confident I didn't understand a word she was saying. Her performance was fully witnessed by a shocked junior chef. Biting my tongue, I continued to lay out the order of beautifully packaged meat on their stainless-steel kitchen bench. The problem seemed to be the small amount of fat we'd added to the mince, something all the other restaurants had insisted on (otherwise the meat tends to be sticky and hard to handle). Finally I retaliated.

'Look, what's the problem? You don't have to buy it.' And I started to load it back into the polystyrene boxes.

The young chef looked more distressed than ever. 'No, no, no. The meat is wonderful,' he said.

'I know,' I replied. 'Tell her.' And I jabbed my finger in the matriarch's direction.

She eventually wrote out a cheque and handed it to me with considerable contempt. With my best accent and a defiant look I took the cheque and said, *'Signora, la ringrazio mille volte. Arrivaderla!'* I began to leave.

'Ah! Scusa, scusa?' she said in a shocked voice. *'Ma signora, lei parla italiano?'*

'Si. Certo!'

She was still saying, *'Scusa, scusa,'* as I left. She wouldn't have bothered had she realised the limit of my Italian vocabulary.

Being belittled by a restaurateur's mother wasn't the worst of it. I hated haggling on the phone over prices. And driving a delivery truck hadn't been in my job description. What I'd experienced in my attempts to unload veal was my first direct encounter with the central crisis of farming, not just during droughts and not just in Australia, but everywhere. There is much discussion about sustainability in agriculture, but the biggest problem is that the prices producers get all over the world aren't enough to sustain them.

When the drought passed, rapturous restaurateurs kept phoning me for more veal, but when I told them that now

I'd need a reasonable price, providing me with at least a hint of a profit, they all said, '*Scusa?*' It was one thing to feel a deep satisfaction from knowing that our meat had found an appreciative audience, but that appreciation wasn't going to be expressed in the form of appropriate payment. So we had to take our veal off their menus.

It doesn't matter what a farmer plants, raises or grows (unless you're a corporation planting a monoculture of cotton across tens of thousands of hectares, sucking streams dry, soaking the soil in chemicals), the chances are they're not going to earn a living. And I don't mean a decent living, let alone a luxurious one, I'm talking about a living. Even the wool barons, our rural aristocrats for generations, are being wiped out by substitute products created in laboratories. It's only a matter of time until that happens to all produce and the technology known as 'pharming' takes off. Phrases like 'protein expression' and 'embryonic micro-injection' will become part of our common vocabulary, just as 'artificial insemination' is today.

Goats with human genes can already be found in US dairy sheds and soon a component of their milk will be in our drugs. One genetically engineered goat, laden with genetic modifications, will earn its proud owners $30 million a year. There's talk about producing steaks in stainless-steel vats in laboratories, steak without cattle. And once the genetic engineers get into full swing, factory farming will take on even more surreal aspects.

Across the world, farmers are being driven off the land in a process that's been going on since the invention of the tractor – a technological development, incidentally, which displaced ten times as many workers as the computer did a century later. In Australia, just a tiny percentage of people is involved in food production. The small fields of France still give the impression of being managed by peasant farmers, but that impression couldn't be further from the truth. Farms are being sold for their houses to be used as weekend retreats, and the surrounding land is often leased to a management company in town.

I get a sense of dread when I walk into a supermarket and see olive oil imported from countries thousands of kilometres away which, even after transport costs and retail mark-ups, sells for 10% of Australian production costs. All of us embarking on this new industry are hoping for a big expansion in the market and for import substitution – but it's only that, a hope. The new olive industry might very well end in ruin, like earlier attempts from the 1860s to the 1960s.

On the first group trip to Europe, Rowie from Merriwa could boast the biggest grove, with over ten thousand trees and intentions to plant another fifty thousand. Paul, the youngest member, also thinking big, has since planted eighty thousand trees at Boundary Bend on the Murray River. But most of us were planning on a less ambitious scale. Twelve months later, when JP went to Europe with the second group, most had large, well-established groves and hyperhubristic plans.

In 1995 Olives Australia, the nursery responsible for this renaissance, had a staff of three; by 2000 they had ninety. Their database sends information to twenty-six thousand households. In 1998 alone they sold a million trees.

'Every year we think it's the peak,' says Julian Archer, one of the directors. 'But it never is.'

Who are all these new olive growers? What were they doing before they planted olives and began calling themselves grove managers, farmers, olive oil makers? I'm meeting so many new recruits I have to add pages to my Filofax, under O for olive people, and write little notes besides their names to remember them: 'interested in bio-dynamics'; 'a hundred trees at Maitland'; 'tall and lanky guy'; 'older man who should know better'.

The couple who lit the first lamp for olives in the Hunter region was the Hunkins, Sharn and Margaret, who've estab-lished a grove at Baerami Creek, one of the most picturesque valleys I've ever seen. While thousands of us are proud to be part of this new wave of olive production, the Hunkins are truly pioneers. Back in 1992, after years managing a nursing home, Sharn started moving slowly into agriculture. He bought a few hectares and began making hay, only to be hit by drought. Then he had an epiphany. He was asked to help move an olive tree from one side of a homestead garden to another. The tree was big and old and magnificent, but the shift didn't help its health. Sharn witnessed its struggle to survive and to his astonishment saw it putting out shoots. He was overwhelmed by the strength and dignity of that tree and it made him start thinking about olives; he began to realise why they have such a role in culture and mythology. Soon he was flying around western New South Wales and Queensland, talking to anyone with the slightest knowledge of these mysterious trees. A year later he and Margaret won a Business Plan of the Year Award for their olive grove proposal.

Sadly the first six hundred trees they planted at their property Mevagissey provided a tasty dietary supplement for the feral deer population, which made nocturnal visits from their home in Wollemi National Park. Faced as well with a sharp reduction in rainfall, the trees expired. But that didn't deter the Hunkins, they planted a further ten thousand.

We all look to Sharn and Margaret for advice. Most of us are terrible fibbers, exaggerating our achievements and our expertise, but Sharn and Margaret tell the truth. They lay bare all their problems during field days, admitting to errors in watering and lay-out; they even reveal their financials. Thanks to their candour and generosity, the rest of us have been given the chance to save ourselves from the same mistakes. But many of us don't. We listen but don't hear. We aren't going to let our dreams be blinded by facts. It's as if there's a drug in the olive oil that's affecting our perceptions. And the Hunkins look on with gentle sadness.

By 1997, after just twelve months of planting, the Hunter Valley had more olive trees in the ground than South Australia, which started planting a century earlier. During the first meetings of the Hunter Olive Association, where I was to spend two years on the committee, you could feel the momentum building and building in the absence of solid information. While we waited for that to materialise through some unimaginable process, we felt no need to constrain our plans, and I was totally swept up in the experience. Food writer Cherry Ripe interviewed me for an article on the erupting olive industry and I said proudly, 'We are the guinea pigs.' When I read it quoted in the newspaper, I wondered why I sounded so proud to be one. And when exactly did I become a gambler?

I remember those early meetings vividly, seated around the Muswellbrook Shire Council's conference table, discussing articles of association, our constitution, bank accounts, newsletter plans, marketing plans, our mission statement. Eight of us, full of enthusiasm, making it up as we went along. Although we were novices, we were light years ahead of those we were to meet in the weeks and months ahead, people from every walk of life – nurses, bankers, agents, teachers, accountants, journalists – all interested in planting a grove but who had never done much more than water a pot plant. Our members came from every walk of life; most of them had worked hard for the money they had, but there were also some brash faces from the city and young people with large inheritances. Printing out the names and addresses of the two hundred members, we learnt that many lived full-time in Sydney, and some were ordering trees before they'd even bought their land.

We began to hold field days, information days, get-togethers, farm walks. The excitement of being part of a new industry, of thinking of beginnings and not of endings, was exhilarating. We were the jolly olive growers.

International prices fluctuate as do currencies, and we were still very unsure about *how* we were going to get our hypothetical fruit from bough to basket. Some would-be growers raised concerns about prices. No land, no groves, no oil, and already an anxiety about no profits. But they were howled down. Maintaining the faith was expected of everyone.

Were we creating an industry? Or was an industry creating us?

What can a government do to help a nascent industry? Not much it seems. I ask some friends in the game and Barry

Jones suggests that 'Political leaders could talk about it as if it mattered.'

Local politicians support any business enterprise in an electorate, they have to, but their capacity to actually do something is virtually nil. Yes, if an olive venture was in a marginal seat there might be a fuss. But to expect any sort of New Deal type of arrangement is absurd.

In *The Lexus and the Olive Tree* (HarperCollins, 1999) Thomas Friedman says there's only one big thing – the market. Otherwise known as God. Friedman's olive tree is there to describe a past that neo-Luddites like us are trying to make the future. The only interest his 'electronic herd' has in agriculture lies in genetic manipulation and the global market. The equity, bond and currency traders wielding their mighty influence don't want to know about digging holes and planting saplings. Nor do the governments that are doing their bidding.

We accepted that it's a friendless world out there, that we were basically on our own. At early association meetings, we discussed how government could best help us. Perhaps they'd fund research? But what research did we need? When you're not sure of the questions, it's hard to find the answers.

Our grove at Elmswood is part of our continuing national history, an attempt to gain wealth from production. Odd how I cling to this belief, when in reality agriculture today represents only 3.3% of our gross domestic product. While the smart money goes to pharming, old-hat farm production satisfies a deeper part of ourselves. Which is why so many of us have avoided the stampede of the electronic herd to remain part of the poor farming herd; there's got to be more than one *Zeitgeist*.

Some see safety in numbers – of trees and investors. So there's been a flurry of big prospectuses that, on cursory inspection, look like tax-avoidance schemes. Private investment costs next to nothing and means revenue forgone for the federal treasury. And the big end of town has the cheek to criticise socialism.

When the big players look like moving in, the response in rural communities is at once joyous and fearful. Does our industry really need these bullies for market presence? They didn't appear at the dawn of the wine industry.

One businessman under perpetual investigation by the National Crime Authority is rumoured to be planting a million trees any moment now. Meanwhile a dozen companies have presented prospectuses with surreal offerings that have investors owning one, ten or a hundred trees – but not the soil they're planted in. Or, alternatively, a bucketful of soil but not the tree. Overnight, entrepreneurs – there's a lovely word – seem to be muscling in, offering olives as an alternative to ostriches and alpacas.

One prospectus on my apocalyptically untidy desk is so glossy it hurts my eyes. Before it disappears into the detritus, I notice photos of smiling, Armani-suited business types. Eighty pages thick, it's filled with machiavellian mumbo-jumbo, with about one fact to every ten fantasies. Even our accountant has trouble deciphering such rubbish, but says, 'All you've got to do is look at the expected headline returns, and this prospectus boasts a 25% average over the twenty-five years of the offer. Not bad after a hefty tax deduction from year one, and the right to claim your own teensy little bit of an awesome olive grove.'

Not all the offers have been taken up by June 30. But that doesn't stop another wave being offered and considered by the Tax Office. Thank God the latter is talking of investigations.

Our friend Jonathan wants to be a crime writer but is still working in finance. He visits the farm almost as frequently as his stressed colleagues visit health clubs. 'It's a lot cheaper at Elmswood,' he tells me. 'Pity about the room service.'

I tell him he'll have to pay for this visit by reading some olive prospectuses. We sit on the verandah as he shuffles through examples of the genre until he delivers his judgement. 'They're not evil. How else do you think the olive industry is going to get real money? Anyone with any sense doesn't invest in agriculture, Patrice. You know that. Why would they? You can get a 100% return on stocks and shares, 200% if you're lucky. More if you're very lucky. You're going to have to accommodate yourself to things you don't like.'

So far, The Barkworth Group has been the most

successful in accessing millions of dollars for olives. I travelled with the founder, Doug Pollard, on one of the overseas olive trips. Doug says he's learnt to interpret tax laws so that they favour him and not the Tax Office, and hopes to snare 35% of the olive oil market in the next few years, envisaging popular brand names backed by big-bucks advertising. Australia doesn't have a great record in promoting brands, and our few successes – like Vegemite, Speedo, Arnott's, Qantas – have a bad habit of falling into foreign ownership. Do Australians really have 'the bottle' to compete in the global market? (John Howard questioned whether Kim Beazley had 'the bottle' for political leadership. But somehow 'bottle' seems ominously appropriate to Australian olive oil.) Olive growers' passions are not without patriotism, at least for the moment. But I wonder which company, which giant company developed with Australian taxpayers' money, will be the first to sell out to an Italian–Spanish consortium?

To avoid being more than a five-second grab in a story about our current account deficit, our industry has to meet many objectives. The environment mustn't be compromised and the consumer mustn't be conned. We've got to produce a truly great product so that the best of it can find a niche in both national and international markets, while the bulk of it provides import replacement. If olive oil is to be a salvation for some areas of rural Australia, our industry needs to have lots of farmers who, with an ecumenical

and democratic spirit, develop a *culture*, not just an industry, as happened in the early days with wine.

A central question arises. How the hell are we going to sell
the stuff? We'll be competing with a billion trees planted
worldwide, from Argentina to France. Even China has
more than twenty million.

'The industry must cut its teeth on the local market,
then export,' says a lanky local lawyer with a small grove.

'Why must it?'

'Because importers in Europe or Asia feel more secure
when an industry has succeeded in its domestic market.'

Which means we have to find a way to sell our extra-
virgin oil to a public that isn't oil literate, a public that has
been happily buying 'pure olive oil' – pure rubbish – for
many years. When drought throughout the Mediterranean
region sent the price of imported oil skyrocketing in the mid-
1990s, consumers seemed content to swap to seed oils like
sunflower and canola. Some people believed that, as a result,
olive oil was repositioned as a prestige product; others
argued that it was priced out of the mass market forever. But
the following year, when olive oil flowed and prices dropped,
the consumers came back. Still nobody can guess what the
consumer reaction will be to higher prices for a better product. True, the provedores are getting $100 a litre for their

top-shelf oils, where the only differential seems to be osten-
tatious packaging. But this is novelty marketing, not the real
thing.

We're not interested in putting our oil into preposterous
bottles. What we'd like to see is a local market developing
along the lines you can still see in rural France, where the
emphasis is on honest food, locally produced. Spend a
minute in the Country Style pavilion at Sydney's Royal
Easter Show and you'll see a massive array of country fare.
And many a rural cafe is now selling local produce; people
are knitting, weaving, sewing, painting and cooking everywhere, helping keep their farms alive and at the same time
providing the basis for a renewal of traditional approaches.
The cooking writers and the TV chefs are calling for a
return to localism.

But as attractive as these ideas are, it's a fantasy to imagine that we can make a profit from Elmswood oil by simply
selling to locals or passers-by. And just having a product,
even a dazzlingly good one, won't guarantee success. Getting it to the people who actually want it is no easy task.
Most boutique products, in food or fashion, fail within a
few years, once the novelty's worn off. Many food producers, faced with the pressure to value add, find themselves
driven indoors to spend their time cooking, phoning, packaging, delivering. And they don't like it.

I live with a marketing man who for twenty years
advised giant corporations on how to sell products and

services. He worked for governments on campaigns to tackle racism and health problems. For fifteen years I've heard first-hand accounts of success and failure, and sometimes the failures have been backed by budgets in the tens of millions. Few of these skills are applicable to a world where farmers hope to sell a few hand-knitted woollen jumpers or jars of jam. Their only hope of making money is that someone, somewhere will buy their little business. Well, it happened to Colonel Sanders.

One well-established olive grower who's been successfully promoting his brand name for years admits he hates selling. Excited after sending off his first batch of oil a decade ago to the local deli and restaurant, he found himself on the road trying to sell to everyone and anyone. As the business grew, so did the need for an ever expanding market and he found himself chasing the rainbow. There was always the hope, the belief that the next big customer would solve his problems. But big customers means the supermarkets. Small shops couldn't buy much and invariably wanted a discount. For every order there were a dozen knock-backs, and as soon as he went near a supermarket, negotiations were ruthless and the margins minuscule. So while he may be able to boast about his oil retailing for $80 a litre, there is little profit.

Every business, to varying degrees, is about selling: ideas, products, services, lies. I should be good at it, God knows I've had loads of experience trying to sell myself as a model. Now there's a profession to toughen the hide! With modelling, as with meat, there's always another body, another carcass, and every model knows the experience of being booked via a cattle call. I hated it. I absolutely loathed it. And there's no difference with meat. Selling is against my nature and I wish I didn't have to do it. But I do.

Even when I ring up butchers who've been buying our meat for years I'm never relaxed. The people we sell to are wonderful and I've nothing but respect for them, but nonetheless when I ring up to confirm an order I half expect to hear, 'Sorry, we don't want your meat any more.'

Some olive growers have sought strength in unity. I'm sure they'd hate to think of it this way, but a co-operative is not unlike a trade union and they have worked in some rural industries. Like 'Commonwealth', the word 'co-operative' sounds anachronistic in these days of cut-throat competition, and those confident of marketing personal boutique brands have been disinclined to join. Yet the word is hopeful. Friendly. Appealing. Even inspirational. It must be better to have a large body of growers sharing resources – harvesters, presses, bottling, marketing – than to have any number of small growers struggling alone at the mercy of corporations owned by remote shareholders. The co-op speaks of localism versus globalism.

Bill Hinchcliff is a man who knows all about the pitfalls of co-operatives. When he first arrived at Elmswood, Rory was absolutely convinced he was Father Christmas.

His snowy beard, his belly laugh proved he'd come directly from the North Pole rather than Ebor, just a few kilometres from Digby and Helen. He's spent most of his business life in a co-operative marketing rice, promoting organic and biodynamic product lines. Overnighting at Elmswood in 1997, he went on to share his knowledge at the first meeting in the Hunter Valley to even consider the idea of a co-op. And he emphasised that the most important act would be to hire a brilliant CEO and let them get on with the job. 'Part-time boards mustn't dictate to full-time management,' he insisted.

Then, for six months in 1998, ten members of the Hunter Olive Association explored the idea of a co-op, producing a strategic plan for processing and marketing, along with a draft constitution. When a public meeting was held in Singleton and people were invited to join, eighty said, 'Yes, thanks very much,' and committed $10 000 each. Now the co-op could be registered. It pressed its first oil two years later, and today is still the only olive co-op in Australia.

Private companies have been springing up in every state, all with the same idea: to create a pipeline from groves to supermarkets. To sell high volumes of quality oil under competitive brand names. They all claim to have the inside running, haul out ancient CVs to prove credentials, and boast of having personal connections to the most influential CEOs, but unfortunately most of these high-ranking executives have long since died or retired to the south of France or the Gold Coast.

Marketing jargon is insufferable. A couple of paragraphs and my mind clouds like unfiltered oil. If I hear another wanker talk about 'benchmark studies', 'psychographics' or 'throughput', I'll scream. Everything is theory, theory, theory. But as with economics, as with everything, outcomes are largely dependent on luck. One thing does become clear: the most successful marketeers are first and foremost illusionists. Take Coca-Cola, undoubtably the most successful brand name of the twentieth century. Once they took the cocaine out of it, it was really just another bottle of sweet water, yet the alchemists at Atlanta turned it into the elixir of youth.

So surely it has to be possible with olive oil? Someone will create a marketing edge through successful illusion and imagery that will cause others to ache with envy.

Follow in the wine industry's footsteps, say the experts and the aspirants. How can we do that? Wine is wine. Oil is oil.

The wine industry is in the midst of a long boom that's seen a few declining rural areas surge forward, creating millionaire grape growers. Please let it happen with oil. Both are value-added products, but where one improves with age (sometimes), the other has to be sold and consumed while it's fresh.

Back in 1966 Dr Max Lake wrote his runaway success, *Classic Wines of Australia*. It was, says Max, a 'book whose time had come', and it sparked a national conversation in wine. Australia already had a wine industry of sorts, started in the nineteenth century, also by medicos, Doctors Penfold and Lindeman. But in 1963, Max, Australia's first hand surgeon, turned his hand to planting grapes in the Hunter, heralding a wine region that would challenge the Barossa. A few of the people who fussed over the vats and drums during Max's first vintages are today amongst our greatest winemakers.

'It was pure lifestyle back then,' says Max. 'Making money didn't enter into it. And we had no idea of becoming a world exporter of wine.' Max and other early winemakers were simply in love with their product. Their passion was to make great wine. With innovations in viticulture giving them a competitive edge, it was only a matter of time until, in Max's words, 'the bean counters moved in'.

Today, with hundreds of people investing their superannuation funds in a block of land and an olive grove, there's an expectation and a need to make a profit. Unlike the early winemakers, many have little interest in the final product or its destiny. This fact was made dramatically evident when the Hunter Olive Association conducted oil tasting courses in 1999 and less than 10% of growers turned up. They'll have to learn, like growers in many sectors of agriculture, that there's no future in just producing a commodity.

With winemaking courses, viticultural expertise and marketing prowess, the wine industry marches on. Will we see tertiary institutions offering courses on growing olives? Will there be degrees in olives? Doctorates in pickling, and post-graduate work in processing? Olive oil doesn't require the same artistry as winemaking but there's no doubt that the perfect batch of olives can be ruined post-harvest. The technical skill in manipulating a press doesn't compare to the skills required for blending, adding yeasts and acids to wine. Olive oil is in essence a simple product, that is its strength. In this day and age, with much food (and some wine) processed beyond recognition, anything unadulterated is valued. Simple, pure, rare products like lobsters, tuna, truffles can command high prices. May biodynamic Australian olive oil be similarly honoured.

Rory is getting sick to death of olives. She loves a song from *Kismet*, 'A Fool Stood Beneath An Olive Tree', and sings it mockingly in my face:

> Why be content with an olive
> when you could have a whole olive tree.
> Why be content to be nothing
> when there's nothing you couldn't be.
> Why be content with just one olive tree

when you could have the whole olive grove.
Why be content with the grove when you could have the
   world.

She makes the following announcement as she packs
her bag for an olive-free week with friends in Sydney:
'Mum, I wish I was an olive tree, then you'd pay more
attention to me.'

I think about this. Am I becoming – or, heaven forbid,
have I already become – one of those mothers too busy to
listen to her child? I wave goodbye. Rory's departure frees
me to drive to, yes, an olive seminar, where I find myself
under an olive tree with a fool. He proudly tells me he's
been working on his CSFs. CSFs?

'Critical Success Factors for good business. I've got
twelve of them.' Oh, please keep quiet. These idiotic
formulations are like the battered junk magazines you can't
help perusing in the doctor's waiting room, wherein men
like him reduce the whole world to formulae. It's bad
enough in business, but spare us personal development
theories in agriculture.

Most high achievers I know have two things in common – madness and luck. They are crazily energetic,
over-excited, doggedly determined mad people. They don't
sit around talking about Critical Success Factors. And I've
yet to find a formula that can cope with droughts, winds,
bogged cars, busted pipes and demanding children.

Rory returns elated, with the news that her friend's mum never cooked dinner once. 'She just made a phone call, Mum, and someone arrived with a pizza. Or dim sims.'

I despair.

'It was cool. Can we do that?'

'No. Now peel these.'

I have a conversation with a local who's planting trees on a corporate mega-grove. He asks me innocently, 'Have your trees lost their leaves yet?'

Olives are evergreen. It emerges that twenty thousand of their trees have died.

The financial pages pontificate about oil. I see headlines like $1 BILLION BILL MAKES REFINING HARDLY WORTH A CRACKER. And OIL INDUSTRY EMBARKS ON ANOTHER BOUT OF RATIONALISING.

Fortunately they're referring to crude oil and corn oil. Oil is on my mind. We're not rationalising yet. We're still in our irrational stage.

Writing on the joys of vegetarianism in an essay called 'Meat Country' in *Granta 52* (Granta Books, 1995), J.M. Coetzee remembers he and his wife being invited to eat with academic colleagues in Texas, where their hosts offered ribs and chicken for dinner, and nothing else.

Nothing else? Just flesh? Anyone who believes meat is doomed to become little more than a flavouring hasn't eaten in Texas. Or, for that matter, Elmswood. For anyone who does physical work for a living, meat is essential. Nothing satisfies deep hunger like meat. Byron, carnivore and poet, rhymed:

> Your labouring people think, beyond all question,
> Beef, veal and mutton better for digestion.

A confession. Before we became beef producers I was verging on vegetarianism myself. Having flirted with the idea as a teenager, influenced by Mahatma Gandhi, I'd walk very quickly past butcher shops on my way to yoga classes. Yoga and vegetarianism went together. Then I gave up modelling, and as soon as you stop worrying about wobbly flesh, it stops wobbling. I lost weight, and with it much of my interest in food. Here at the farm, where I really make demands on my body, my body demands meat, and meat demands vegetables. And vegetables demand olive oil.

Georges Perec wrote a novel without using the letter 'e' but I couldn't write this book without paying tribute to the doyenne of food writers, Elizabeth David. When I was a student at St Aloysius College, I displayed no talent for French. Consequently, I was placed in the dummies' class where the focus was on French culture rather than the language. If we couldn't progress past the conjugation of 'to be', we could at least appreciate soufflé! Although a dictionary was kept on hand for reference, our new text became Elizabeth David's *French Provincial Cooking*. I still have my dog-eared, food-stained Penguin edition bound in clear plastic with copious amounts of Sellotape. Amongst our teacher's innovations was her decree that French homework would involve trying out the odd French recipe.

My mother and I found Mrs David's pictureless book *très difficile*. Neither of us had any idea how the food should look, let alone taste, so the homework I returned to the dummies' class was rarely edible. Nonetheless those discussions about local ingredients in provincial France were my first introduction to the gourmet world, and to olives. In one class we were introduced to the salty little things, shown how to chew them and, as elegantly as possible, spit out the pips. On another occasion we mixed olive oil with lemon juice and poured it over lettuce leaves. I thought nothing could ruin a lettuce more.

By the time I was born, Mrs David had already published *A Book of Mediterranean Food* (1950), *French Country Cooking* (1951), *Italian Food* (1954), *Summer Cooking* (1955), and had begun her legendary columns for British

Vogue. In 1992 I was preparing various forms of goo for Rory when news came that she'd died. The phone rang hot with foodie mates ululating in grief. For months you couldn't pick up a food journal without another writer claiming an intimate lifelong friendship with Liz: 'The time I called in for coffee . . . ' 'Liz made me a cake . . . '

Yet as late as the 1965 edition of *A Book of Mediterranean Food*, olives get only one mention in Mrs David's index. She refers us to Lawrence Durrell, who on 10 January 1938 in *Prospero's Cell* wrote:

> The whole Mediterranean – the sculptures, the palms, the gold beads, the bearded heroes, the wine, the ideas, the ships, the moonlight, the winged gorgons, the bronze men, the philosophers – all of it seems to rise in the sour, pungent taste of these black olives between the teeth. A taste older than meat, older than wine. A taste as old as cold water.

This passage is oft quoted and deserves to be, as it perfectly sums up the rise of sensual flavour and the cultural connotations of an apparently humble fruit. However, Durrell's description is emphatically masculine – naturally so perhaps, since in the European world language is defined by gender – and consequently paints only half the picture.

Mrs David writes that green olives which are to be served with cocktails or as hors-d'oeuvres:

[...] are better bought by the pound, not in bottles; prepare them in this way, as they do in Marseille.

Choose the small, oblong French or Greek olives. In each olive make an incision with a knife, and put them in layers in a jar with some pieces of cut garlic and 2 or 3 stalks of thyme, and a small piece of chilli pepper, fill the jars up with olive oil, and cover them. In this way they are stored for months.

Whilst we might learn some discernment from Mrs David, her recipe raises new questions. This is no way to cure olives, this is what to do with them after you've purchased them pickled.

Pickling is an art in itself. If you buy an over-salted batch, or olives that have been floating in poor-quality vinegar or brine, they'll never be any good. Fortunately, finding pickled olives of good quality isn't as difficult as it used to be. One of Sydney's snootier provedores sells over fifteen varieties decanted into ceramic bowls, while an entirely different assortment in exotic jars lines the shelves. I always buy too many of them – there's never enough room in the fridge. But what I like best is to tip out a jar of olives I've pickled myself. They're like jewels to be eaten, not something sickly sweet or overcoloured, but black pearls, or green pearls.

Whole libraries are now dedicated to the virtues of olives and olive oil. Among the better books are *Olive Oil:*

From Tree to Table by Peggy Knickerbocker; *Saffron, Garlic &* *Olives* by Loukie Werle; *Feast of the Olive* by Maggie Blyth Klein; *The Essential Olive Oil Companion* by Anne Dolamore. The International Olive Oil Council has published many tomes about olives but *The Olive in Mediterranean Cooking* is especially good.

Almost every one of these books waxes lyrical about olive tapenade, the paste I now keep on hand as I once did pesto. One rainy afternoon I checked all my cookbooks and discovered that the basic ingredients for olive tapenade are always the same: black or green olives, but preferably black, anchovies, capers and extra-virgin olive oil. Each recipe varies the amounts and then suggests different additions: lemon zest, fresh oregano, rosemary or parsley. It's best to make it differently every time anyway. I make loads of it. It keeps well in the fridge and can be tossed into pasta, spread on bread, smeared on fish, and it makes a rich dark risotto to serve with char-grilled capsicums.

If you don't own one, buy an olive pitter. If you've got a six-year-old, buy one as a Christmas present. Rory loves pitting olives and they also work on cherries. When Rory announces she wants to do a 'food experiment', I produce the pitter and a fresh jar of olives, and *voilà!* I've saved the kitchen from mass destruction for another day. When her efforts with the olive pitter have been particularly energetic and I've filled the fridge with tapenade, it's time to make olive bread. I first encountered this at the Bayswater

Brasserie in Kings Cross in the mid-eighties, and I remember the restaurant being abuzz with chatter about this new and exciting *pane*, as challenging a taste as the first munch of garlic bread a few decades earlier.

It might affront the puritans who like whole pitted olives evenly punctuating the dough, but I make olive bread in the bread machine. My purple bread, aubergine to the modern colourist, comes out with olive flecks rather than whole fruit. If I'm the only one eating, I use a coarse-ground wheat to make an even darker, browner, dirtier looking loaf; otherwise I use an organic flour. The bread is simple to make: a packet of yeast, three cups of plain flour, one tablespoon of extra-virgin olive oil, salt, and 120 millilitres of water. This makes a fairly dry dough. When the machine bips after fifteen minutes, add the pitted olives. Otherwise throw them in just before the last knead. Before I had a supply of my own home-pickled olives I used organic black ones. Wash them first to remove traces of the brine, pip them, then squeeze out the excess moisture before adding them to the dough. If you use fresh Kalamatas, the olive flesh is firmer and doesn't colour the dough as much. But purple bread looks great grilled, perfect to plonk goat's cheese on. The final touch: a drizzle of more green olive oil.

Although there are good-quality butters now available, both properly cultured and unsalted, it's hard to ignore all the evidence that olive oil is better for you. Look at the healthy skin of Italian men – is it really all in their genes, or is their secret cosmetic a diet rich in olive oil? Olive oil is a monounsaturated fat. It contains tocopherols (Vitamin E), with antioxidant properties.

You can substitute olive oil for butter in most recipes. Generally a cup of butter – or 185 grams if you're fussy – can be replaced by three-quarters of a cup of oil. I hate using kitchen scales, except when making jam, so all my recipes are instantly converted to cup and spoon measurements. Any bread, including a sweet loaf, is improved with olive oil, and cakes are moister. Even very fresh green extra-virgin oil won't taint the flavour of a cake, but while the taste remains the same, the nutrition is very different because you've dramatically reduced the cholesterol and saturated fat content. Poppyseed cake, a lunchbox favourite, normally uses loads of milk and butter, but it's even more successful with organic soy milk and extra-virgin olive oil.

While my mother didn't care for it, she cooked uncomplainingly. Because of her 'eat to live, not live to eat' philosophy, her meals were unashamedly if not elegantly simple meat-and-three-veg dishes. There was some variation in the vegetables, but the meals were always presented on the same plain blue plates, as if she'd been inspired by Japanese sashimi chefs and Zen. Her objective, as she explained years later, was simply to maximise nutrition, not make art on a plate. But in her own way she did just that:

'Have a vegetable of every colour and you can't go wrong.' I carry on my mother's kitchen traditions at Elmswood, but with the many more ingredients that are available today.

Getting the hang of a country kitchen takes time. It's not so much a question of what to cook as what to do with 20 kilograms of cucumbers, or 100 kilograms of green olives. A thousand green tomatoes at the end of the season. Would you like a pumpkin? You would? Great! Here, take ten. One year Phillip took a truckload of pumpkins back to Sydney, thrusting them into everyone's arms.

While their editorials infuriate me, rural newspapers provide a good source of recipes to be cut out and stuffed in an untidy drawer. But most features on ingredients respond to gluts in the market and come too late for country chefs, so I keep last year's recipes in a place where I can't find them, to be synchronised with my crops. Just when we need a break from stuffing ourselves with apricots, the peaches ripen overnight, forcing us to move the chairs beneath the trees to eat them all before the birds do. The figs are so much more considerate. When I come back from a job, I walk straight to the tree, tear open a dozen and enjoy the juicy flesh, throwing the skins aside. In 1999 our fig crop was so prolific, half the tree collapsed. That didn't stop us picking at least a hundred bucketfuls. Fortunately figs don't ripen all at once and can be enjoyed progressively, fresh or cooked.

One year I poured loads of our honey onto opened figs

and placed them in a slow oven for a few hours. Some we ate straight away, while others were spread over tarts layered with mascarpone.

By the time I pick the last fig in March I'm usually glad I won't be eating them for another year.

Your meat-pie-and-biscuit type of man, Phillip is too easy to please. When I don't feel like cooking and want inspiration I ask him, 'Would you like anything in particular?'

'Whatever you feel like.'

Whatever isn't helpful. But then few men are genuinely content with cheese on toast for dinner.

The nuns at St Joseph's, the Kurralta Park branch of the Holy Roman Church, emphasised the sin of gluttony. To the sin of gluttony, add the sin of pretension.

When I was a model, meals were often stressful. Do I dare eat this? Could I possibly eat that? I was living in New York and befriended David, who'd made a reputation photographing the nine hundred bloated corpses in a Guyana jungle clearing, the poisoned victims of Jim Jones's fanaticism. With these appalling images he hit the big time. He began an affair with a member of the Shah of Iran's family, and they shacked up at a quirky hotel called the Sherry Netherland on Fifth Avenue. David invited a group of us to watch the Superbowl there. Football is bad enough, but I knew I was in for a very difficult afternoon when the conversation turned to how the 'poor Shah' was being maltreated, how he was 'having such trouble getting visas'.

Beer and popcorn were served during quarter-time. But at half-time Her Majesty ordered caesar salad. I knew a little about Iranian politics, but I knew nothing about caesar salad. Room service delivered our six salads – torn cos lettuce leaves, chunky fried bacon, brown croutons and large slivers of parmesan – each beautifully presented with its own silver cover. Her Royal Highness lifted the lid off one, let out a scream, and ran to the door to catch the waiter.

'Take them back!'

Why?

'The dressing has already been tossed!'

The waiter wilted.

'I want fresh dressing mixed here so I can see.'

She turned to us, exasperated. 'Honestly! These days!' Moments later the head chef arrived with new salads and the dressing ingredients on the side, including the essential fresh egg, and proceeded to mix and toss. After tasting the food, Her Majesty allowed him to leave. Leaving my appetite destroyed. My first caesar salad tasting awful. Ever since I've remained uneasy about fussing over food.

I'm into nutrition, not the exquisite gourmet experience.

I'm swotting up on olive culture and the information is as choked with flotsam as flooded waters. There's a rush and disturbance, at times a violent momentum, as each fact, opinion or theory joins the maelstrom. But amidst all of it is knowledge that grows like love.

Thoughts flow backwards too, as much as forwards. I phone Diana, my first best friend in Kurralta Park over thirty years ago, and tell her I'm coming to Adelaide.

'Phillip is giving a speech and I'm visiting olive groves.'

'My ex-lover knows about olives,' Diana says, as vibrant as ever. She's now a potter living a rich personal and professional life near a beach south of Adelaide. 'You must call him.' And she reads out his number.

When I get there I call. 'Is that Michael Burr? I'm a friend of Diana's . . . ' And I tell him my story.

Later, sitting in his home (and medical practice, Michael too is a doctor) eating his olives, tasting his oil as if it were wine, my innocent enthusiasms are confronted by tales of misadventure and warnings of pitfalls. Michael, however, is as enthusiastic as I am.

The following day Phillip and I drive out past ruins of sandstone houses, over dry creekbeds to Michael's beloved Beetaloo, an early nineteenth-century house surrounded by his olive grove. This patch of land has been a passion he's shared with friends for two decades. An oasis it isn't. It has the sort of tough beauty you'd expect to find in Calabria. On a blindingly bright South Australian day, it's cool and dark inside the sandstone. On the wall are pictures of Michael's ex-lovers, mainly naked, including Diana taking a bath in the moonlight. I look around and there's the wrought-iron bath baking in the sun, its claws gripping at the dust. I hardly ever see Diana these days – a phone chat, a birthday card – and here she is in all her voluptuousness, on the wall of a stone house at Beetaloo. The circles of life.

Michael, who embodies his olive ethos, clearly thrives on adversity. A physician who cannot heal himself, he's suffering from Parkinson's disease. Suffering? No, that's not the right word. He's fascinated by it. (Years after this visit he says to me, 'It's the most extraordinary disease, although I'd enjoy understanding it more if it wasn't happening to me.') Just as the olive tree has no time for self-pity, Michael has no time to dwell on mortality. He's far too alive for that. Somehow the name Burr is perfect for him, suggesting his qualities of tenacity and determination. His body is as trim and strong as the trees in his grove, and his speech is slow and deliberate, as if every syllable is being weighed and considered. As indeed it is. He explains that Parkinson's is affecting his vocabulary and syntax and he has to construct each sentence slowly in his head before he can begin to deliver it.

Nothing is easy for Michael. But nothing stops him from finding joy in life. For example, he is writing a book, a mighty compilation of all his thoughts and ideas about olives. There are papers and books all over the benches and tables. (Years later I buy a bound edition of *Australian Olives: A Guide for Growers and Producers of Virgin Oils*. Self-published and constantly revised, it is in my opinion the most important contribution to Australian olive literature.) He's an inspiration as a human being and something of a genius as an orchardist. He's also very funny. He takes us past the bath, around a water tank, and into a shed where an odd-looking machine is surrounded by what look to be hundreds of pizza bases. These turn out to be the filter mats, and the machine an olive press. It's like the scene in *2001: A Space Odyssey* when they first encounter the mysterious singing obelisk. Michael's excitement about this weird device is infectious and we spend the next hour in animated discussion. Phillip wonders off to peruse the nude photos of Michael's old lovers.

Eventually, in 1999, Michael comes to Elmswood, driving alone from Wagga Wagga in one long haul. At daybreak I tiptoe down the stairs expecting him to be asleep in the guest bedroom, but it's empty. He's outside wandering about in his sarong and T-shirt, and explains that it was so dark when he arrived he wasn't sure he was at the right place, so to be on the safe side he parked in the garage and slept in his car.

Yes, this is the right place. He takes a brown silk dressing gown from his car and we go inside to sip tea. It's January and burning hot by nine, so together with JP and Matthew we venture to the grove before the heat ruins the day. I want his opinion on everything. The Leccino look better than the Correggiola, don't they? Is this soil going to be too heavy? Why are these leaves a different shade of green? Michael, just tell me *everything*. I'm wearing gum boots, protection against snakes and seed heads. Michael stands next to me in slip-ons and silk, oblivious to the scratching plants around him. He has a lot to say. Some of the smaller trees that reshooted after being burned from frost look different. 'It's the immature growth,' he says, snipping off one branch and holding it up against another. 'These immature trees will take ten years to fruit. Perhaps you should pull them out?'

Near the garage are the last hundred Frantoio waiting to be planted. I point to a yellowing leaf. 'What do you think about this?'

'Leaves can drop off, it's usually nothing.' But then on closer inspection he gets excited. 'This is olive lace bug!' he shouts. My blood freezes. 'Look!' He turns the leaf over. 'Yes, definitely. See, that's their poo. I need a photo of this.'

I squint closely at the poo. He rushes back to the garage, dives into the rubble of his car, produces a camera and rushes back, dressing gown flapping.

'How will you get rid of it without chemicals?' he asks, expecting an intelligent answer.

'I haven't the faintest idea.'

Being told your trees have a disease is like being told your child has a disability you hadn't noticed.

Later, on the patio, Michael opens up his laptop, attends to urgent correspondence and brushes aside my concern about lace bugs. Michael is inured to calamity and simply smiles soothingly. He's already thinking of the next grove and the next calamity. A cup of tea and he's off, and I've still got a thousand other questions.

That night, Rory struggles with Phillip's massive seventeenth-century telescope, trying to find the almost full moon. It's so close in the lens that she stretches out her other arm as if to touch the craters. Before going to bed we lie on the cool dry grass and gaze at the vast, scintillating galaxy. There's so much to tend to down here, but our eyes are heavenward and we see the red and green navigation lights of a plane heading south.

'Are the stars alive, Mum?'

'Yes. In their way.'

'Where's the Southern Cross?'

I show her.

'What's south?'

Geologist Professor John Roberts from the University of New South Wales once came to Elmswood to collect samples of volcanic rocks that preserve the old north–south in their molecular alignment. Rocks that remember the past. John explained that the world's magnetic field flip-flops or reverses, the North Pole becoming the South Pole – the world doesn't actually turn upside down. I tell Rory that one volcanic rock collected near our highest peak has been dated, using uranium–lead isotopes, at 319 million years. She sighs a deep sigh, and in that second sees a shooting star. But as I look at the sky's million lights, all I can see is a million lace bugs.

Too depressed to tackle them I wait another few days, resenting the time I must spend boning up on a bug that promises to turn leaves into lace, sap all the nutrients and eventually kill the plant. 'Your trees will definitely die,' a grower tells me gleefully, 'unless you spray them *immediately*.' What with? Chemicals of course.

These trees aren't even in the ground and already they need a medical prescription? I remind myself that plants tend to recover from insect attacks, just as humans recover from illness, but is this a sore throat or a cancer? I'm an atheist who seeks a blessing, so I decide to baptise the trees, just in case. These trees are from a commercial nursery in Western Australia and are little more than six months old. Taken from cuttings and pushed along in a hothouse, their entire life has been a diet of artificial fertilisers. Now I'm expecting these trees to overcome their first bug attack without the aid of any drug, yet they've never even been required to obtain a nutrient naturally, via humus. I know this is a big ask.

What I'm about to do exposes my level of panic. I mix olive oil and water in a small watering can, shake it and spray it over the yellowed leaves. It's entirely intuitive but I'm hoping it will produce a varnish that might protect the leaves from further attack. A day later I brew a weak tea from our biodynamic compost and spray the plants with it, again in the hope of providing extra nutrients. I place compost on top of each pot, pressing it down until it looks like olive tapenade and good enough to eat. Moving them to a sunny position near the garden tap, I make a kind of hospital for them, hoping it isn't, inadvertently, a hospice. What they probably need most of all is the support of our biodynamic soil, but they'll have to wait for that.

Days pass and the winged beasts refuse to take the hint and leave, until, one afternoon, after the lightest sun shower, it seems as though the trees themselves take a deep breath and simply blow the bugs away. The leaves darken, filling with life.

And once they're planted out no one will ever know their sickly start in life.

It's steaming hot and we're sitting on the verandah waiting for Phillip's Aunty Pat to arrive with her dog Chip. I've been keen to meet Pat Fraser because Phillip's first introduction to his aunt, two years older than he, is the sort of family yarn buried in memory.

Phillip tells me that Richard Attenborough's film *Chaplin* begins with a crowded backstage scene dominated by a curvaceous woman in white tights mustering a small herd of trained seals towards the footlights. This memorable performer was Phillip's paternal grandmother. She left her seal-training act to became a hand-colourist of motion film, painting each frame with little brushes. Her husband was killed in Gallipoli and not long afterwards she met Tom Callaway from Warracknabeal, in Victoria, while he was holidaying in England. He offered his hand in marriage, and as soon as she could dump her son Charles (Phillip's father) onto her sister, she was off. Years later, when Charles turned sixteen, he came out to Australia hoping for a reconciliation with his mother and was promptly sent to work in Melbourne. Seeking respectability, he ultimately became a Congregational minister and, according to Phillip, continued to get the cold shoulder from his mother. Charles, divorced from Phillip's mother Sylvia, decided to try again and presented thirteen-year-old Phillip at Warracknabeal in the hope of a warm welcome.

On their arrival in town Phillip remembers seeing the most beautiful girl running along the footpath. To his astonishment, this vision of loveliness turned out to be his aunt, the twelve-year-old adopted daughter of the Callaways.

'Pat, now this is your nephew Phillip. Phillip, this is your Aunty Pat.'

Sitting upright in his best clothes, Phillip saw that his grandma still detested her son, cared less for him and couldn't wait for them to leave. Nonetheless, the day was a success of sorts, for Phillip had met Pat.

Now a widow, with a tribe of children and grand-children, Pat is one of those people who keeps friends and family informed of births, deaths, marriages and adventures through an annual report attached to the Christmas card. Pat is a passionate supporter of the ALP and during the Kennett era her annual reports were full of rage and fury. Phillip once thanked Jeff Kennett for keeping his mother alive, claiming that it was only Sylvia's incandescent loathing of him, manifested in streams of abuse directed at the nightly news, that kept her going. So it is with Pat, who regards the malignancy of the casino culture as the lowest ebb in Victoria's political life. She has, however, been able to soothe herself with music, investing part of her tiny capital in a suburban music cafe. Playing the piano remains a deep pleasure, and she tells of a childhood scene where, at the Callaways' piano, she vowed to become a great pianist.

Forty years after she first met Phillip and hours late, Aunty Pat arrives at Elmswood. So Phillip's grandmother was your mother! I think to myself. And I spend the next couple of days trying to reconstruct some of the more mysterious passages in Pat's life, cross-examining her about Phillip's childhood and once again stumbling across a connection to olives. Just as Diana led me to Michael Burr, Pat leads me to Phil Henry, an old friend of hers who for twenty-one years was the general manager of Oliveholme.

'I've never heard of it,' I say.

'You must have,' insists Pat as she writes out his phone number. 'It was a huge grove at Robinvale. The biggest in Australia.'

'What do you mean, was? What happened to it?'

'They pulled the trees out, I think.'

I don't like hearing stories about groves being grubbed, but that's exactly what happened in the eighties to Olive-holme's 80 hectares of oil trees, which produced up to 90 000 litres in a good year, and the 120 hectares of table olive trees that produced 1000 tonnes of fruit. And why? Because Oliveholme couldn't make a profit.

'Olives aren't easy,' Phil Henry says on the phone. Despite the fact that his olive trees were Correggiola, the favoured oil variety, and despite his having had an olive press on site, and despite selling all the oil that was produced in tins at the farm gate, they still couldn't get the economics right.

Now, a little over a decade later, the same land is again being planted with olives. No sooner had I discovered Phil Henry and his twenty-one years of experience than the whole industry did. Now his phone never stops ringing.

There's more than mateship to the history of the outback. Legends abound of drovers' wives and pioneer women, and of women abused by men whom not even celebrators of mateship like Henry Lawson could defend. 'Squeaker's Mate' is one of Australia's grimmest tales, about the wife of a timber cutter who is dumped in an outhouse after she is paralysed by a falling bough. Through the implacable power of her hatred, she first haunts and then terrorises the new mate that Squeaker brings to their slab hut. Barbara Baynton (1857–1929) wrote the story in the 1890s.

Baynton could write 'Squeaker's Mate' because she'd lived a similar life. Her husband was an alcoholic and an adulterer who left her for months on end. After giving birth to her second child, she discovered him in bed with her young niece. Baynton rescued herself and her children from this miserable existence, leaving her husband so he could shack up with her niece, whom he also abused and subsequently committed to a psychiatric hospital where she died.

The actor Penne Hackforth-Jones is Baynton's great-granddaughter and biographer. Visiting a town near Gundy where Baynton had lived with her husband, she asked the locals what, if anything, they knew of her and was appalled to hear her recalled as 'that nasty, go-getting woman'.

Yes, local memories have Baynton as the bitch. How dare she leave her husband!

Baynton remarried, started writing, had her fiction praised to the heavens by the likes of H.G. Wells, considerably influenced the young Patrick White, and died a rich woman.

But she'd left her husband.

It's the pioneer woman standing by her man, helping clear the land and raise the children, who remains the approved figure in the rural landscape. In truth, this image represents a sizeable fraud, for while rural women are once more asserting themselves – in autobiographies, in contests like Rural Woman of the Year, in profile pieces in *The Land* and *The Weekly Times* – they are most likely to succeed professionally when their men have gone. Most success stories follow when women get divorced or, more often, are widowed. Few women acquire agricultural businesses on their own, or become directors of rural companies while young or still married. In the upper echelons of rural enterprises, and on the advisory boards of state and federal organisations, women are as few and far between as trees on the Nullarbor. Women didn't venture out on horseback to snatch land grants a hundred and fifty years ago and they don't have the same motives or determination to simply make money from the land today. Our stories are still, by and large, domestic ones.

Feminists used to ask whether women in politics would produce a different or better governance. I ask myself similar questions about the world I've chosen. Do women mutilate the landscape the way men did and do? Are women as ruthlessly exploitative? Or do our famous nurturing qualities make us accept the land's limitations more readily? We'll have some indications in our olive industry, where the management of groves is overwhelmingly dominated by women. And many I know care for their trees the way they care for their children.

JP drives to Ebor to check on the agisted cattle. The 1997/98 drought, now officially declared in the Hunter Valley, is yet to reach the Northern Tablelands. We hope the cattle can remain there until April.

The only good thing about drought is that weeds don't grow, and we're spared hours of hoeing and slashing, which time is now needed for feeding out silage and hay and planting more olives. The ground is getting harder and harder, the river so low we can only pump to the tank for a few hours each day. Irrigation is out of the question. The garden is alive but a wreck. I let the chooks out around noon and they race to scratch earth shadowed by Monsieur Tillier, my favourite rose. Soon they'll probably go in the other direction and start scratching around the olives. Each day is interminable.

Work expands to fill available time and space. My dad spent as much time fussing in his suburban shed as JP does on a thousand hectares, or I do in our olive grove. No matter how much time I allow for a job, it's never enough, but planting trees is, for all the effort, a great joy. Knowing they can have a life longer than ours, knowing that someone else will be enjoying their old age and hopefully caring for them, as we do the hundred-year-old *Celtis occidentalis* in front of the homestead. They can live for six hundred years, the tree surgeon tells me as he saws off branches that are rubbing the guttering. Six hundred years? Will the house still be standing then? And olives can live for thousands.

This thirsty summer our grove is a shimmer of silver. It

strobes like a disco. The glare is so harsh you need the sun close to the horizon before you can discern colour. The olive trees look greener and happier as night falls. They seem to respond to the moon, which biodynamic farmers use to help understand the behaviour of plants. On every continent, peasant farmers still use the moon as a sowing guide, always knowing where the moon is in its cycle, whether it be near or far, apogee or perigee. Even olives that have been bold specimens of good health sometimes look sick, less vibrant, as the moon wanes. The first few times we noticed it we thought they were under attack: Not again! But as the moon cycle moves on, the trees regain their energy. Now, whenever I suspect a problem, I think of the moon. And I don't like people to visit the grove while the moon wanes.

Phillip's lifelong friend, the painter Joy Peck, regularly visits from Melbourne. Each time she brings a gift. One of the first was an olive tree, a Verdale that I planted in the low garden between an oak and a ginkgo. Although neglected, it's survived. Now old enough to fruit, it has a fistful of jasper beads dangling in the wind. The tree is pubescent. Winds shrivel the fruit. I bring water and they fill out again. There's something sexual about olives and their response.

I've got too close to snakes for my own liking. A tall cherry blossom was *in extremis* and I was dragging the hose towards it, past a wisteria that winds around a balustrade. There, next to my foot, centimetres from a bare ankle, was a fat brown snake, neatly coiled, its head lifted for attack, its tongue flicking its forked tip. Snakes look at you like no other creature. We stare at each other for far too long, as if we're being polite, before I make the first move, stepping backwards, hose in my hand. The snake relaxes and slithers off. I can't get the creature's *stare* out of my head. When JP arrives he takes a hoe and goes searching without success.

'Did it give you the eye?' JP asks.

'Yes.'

JP knows what I'm feeling. Terror. A brush with death.

Then, minutes later, Rory is in the pool and calls out, as she's been taught, 'Snake alert! Snake alert!' Swimming around with her is a thin, red-bellied black. JP picks up the pool scooper and flicks it out.

I always tell city kids what to do when they see one. Stop. Look at it. Is it black, brown, white? Does it have stripes? Keep still for a moment, then very carefully step back. Then and only then start running. Run to an adult and tell them.

Another time, Keith and I were working in the grove when he called out, 'Snake!' An immense brown had been sleeping where he was about to weed. Disturbed, it was very cranky. Yet Keith was able to almost hypnotise it. He took off his hat, bent down and trembled it in front of the snake's head, walking backwards, making it dance towards him, away from where I was working. Keith was half snake charmer, half bullfighter.

The days are so steamy you could drink the air. If only it would rain.

I order timber stakes from the sawmill, 50 millimetres thick and 2.25 metres long. The cane stakes have failed the wind test. Each time a gale blows, more trees lean over. I resent the waste of effort, we should have used decent stakes from the beginning. The new ones are so long and heavy I can only carry two at a time. They splinter my hands easily, and don't fit in the back of my Mazda. They're too long to be hammered in. JP uses a steel gadget that slides over the stake like a metal sock, and with two or three bangs he has it 25 centimetres into the ground. I can't even lift the steel gadget up over the stake and don't have the muscles to thump it. So JP puts them in and I retie the trees.

Up and down the rows we go. A hundred stakes in and fourteen hundred to go. It's a slow job as we must assess each tree. If it's firm and straight enough, we leave it.

This week has tried our nerves. Besides the build-up of heat, dry storms have centred on Elmswood. Neighbours don't get a flicker of wind but our olive grove cops the lot.

There's thunder, there's lightning, but there's no rain. Next morning the trees we'd okayed are horizontal and have to be restaked and tied.

Every tree needs fine-tuning. A little weeding, a hare guard repositioned, more mulch spread, an invading thistle chipped away, redundant green tape picked up. Originally we'd used a staple gun, designed for nursery use, to attach the trees to the stakes. While it made the grove look very professional, the stapling only lasted a few weeks. As soon as a tree began to show some character and actually grow, or the winds arrived to challenge them, the staple snapped off. Then the trees played an irritating game of hide in the grass, and we had to spend hours disentangling them. Now we cut up orange twine from the hay bales and tie them firmly to the stake. Cutting the twine into 30-centimetre strips is the sort of job you do when you can't be bothered doing anything else.

A proud Keith arrives straight from Glenbawn Dam with fresh fish. Bream and baked chips for dinner. Delicious. Mum, Rory and I sit outside and watch stormclouds move towards us. The sky is blue around us, black beyond. The poplars rustle. I ignore the few leaves floating on the pool and go inside to watch Ian Parmenter make olive bread before the news headlines. No sooner have I sat down when Rory rushes in. 'It's a blower, Mum! Come and watch!' Storms instil wild excitement in children and dogs. Rory begins racing around, peering from this window and that, while Rosie and Molly cower under the kitchen table. Now the thick boughs of the *Celtis* and deodar are making shapes that look as if all their branches will be torn from the trunks. I hate to think about the olives. Simultaneously, Mum, Rory, the two dogs, the birds and I squeal as thunder claps overhead. The house rocks. There's a musical deluge as loud as a choir of baritones on the roof.

A builder had been demolishing part of the laundry that day and I'd emptied cupboards and piled the contents all over the patio. The patio is a bad place to be if it rains hard. It floods, often sending a river into the house. It's even worse when crowded with new jars for honey, rag bags, honey frames, eskies, cushions, ironing board and iron, all of which are now getting soaked. I need a truckload of newspapers to make levees to keep the water out of the house and kitchen, but discover that Phillip has removed the lot in one of his clean-ups. I pick up everything I can, piling things on top of the fridge and tossing down towels that form an inadequate barrier against the rising water.

Out of the corner of my eye I glimpse Mum standing behind the door, clearly distressed. An arrow of fear. She's been unable to light her cigarette and stands there erect, matches in one hand, wet translucent cigarette in the other. She steps forward and yells, 'I'm going to bed.'

'But Mum, I can't open the door. I'll flood the hallway. Let me make you comfortable here.'

Through the downpour I guide her to the kitchen table, find some new matches and a dry cigarette and light up for her. Puff, puff. I wish smoking were good for you. Hand shaking, she puts the white tube of tobacco to her lips. I slide the ashtray closer. Sensing the tension of the moment, Rory recalls the usefulness of music, like the 'Nearer My God To Thee' scene in *Titanic*, and shouts over the thunder of rain.

'Nonna. I'll play the violin.' Lifting her instrument from the case she plays 'Twinkle Twinkle Little Star' over and over again.

'Does it sound like a Stradivarius, Nonna?'

'Just like it, dear.'

The music has worked. Mum is smiling again, and we settle down to enjoy the storm as it moves around the house. The clouds are so low, it's raining horizontally. A showering of knives that wets everything. The power goes off. Where are those candles? Why did I leave the torch upstairs? Why care now? The towel levy breaks; water spreads out around our ankles, over the patio, into the laundry, kitchen, hallway. And what about the olives?

It's never boring on a farm.

Once the drought breaks, the rains keep coming. Just days before, we'd put in three expensive tensiometers across the grove to help us measure moisture and calculate a more accurate water regime. Now they record the obvious. They tell us the grove is saturated.

Olives have great tenacity and survive in some of the harshest landscapes on earth. It's a cruel thought that in some sections of planting, the high soil fertility may actually be spoiling the trees – these are the areas that hold the most moisture.

We don't bring the cattle back from Ebor straight away. We let the pasture recover and spray it with 500.

Twelve months after planting we can see the grove creating its grid over the hillside. You can't stand on the edge of it and see it in its entirety; it doesn't look like much until you walk from one end to the next, up the hillside, around the bend, up and down a rock-strewn gully and behind the shearing shed, then it looks like a grove.

By introducing greater vegetative complexity to Elmswood, we seem to make every hectare larger. It's like the wilds at the back of the property where nature fills every hillside and gully with botanic profusion. People think of emptiness as feeling large, but it's detail that magnifies the experience.

As part of an organic food conference in South Australia, we visited a 15-hectare farm near Gawler based on the permaculture (permanent + agriculture) principles of the irascible Bill Mollison. Ornamental shade and fruit trees were blended with crops, vegetables and flowers. Fifteen hectares? It felt like hundreds.

As we intensify planting and activity around the farm, we change the entire dimensions and intention of the place. Big paddocks might make a place look important, yet it feels less productive. Getting the proportions right has always been an important factor, both in gardening and farming.

Olive groves are changing the feel and productivity of landscape across the state. It's inevitable that some of the trees will go feral, as they did in South Australia. There's already a proliferation in the forests around Inverell, where in the industrial park an olive press has been erected. Symbolising the hopes of an entire industry, this giant meccano set fills an entire building. It's very impressive, promising to convert 1200 kilograms of fruit per hour into oil.

Olives Australia tells us of portable olive pressing machines that can fit into a garage and process 50 to 250 kilograms an hour. They offer to lend us one for an open day at Elmswood.

We ask local growers if they have fruit. They do. Not a lot, but some. And they're very excited at the thought of having it pressed. We agree on a date. We book the machine.

There are rumours of an old neglected olive grove near Scone. JP and I go searching, our eyes seeking a hint of the familiar grey-green leaves. We notice grey-leaved trees and suspect callistemons, but on closer inspection realise they're tall healthy olives sharing a gully with eucalypts. Then, everywhere we turn we see them, wild happy, naturalised. Their willowing shimmer has an Australian cadence – like our humour, dry and understated. That they can't be imprisoned is a good sign and a bad sign.

Finally, beyond a new vineyard, past cattle and sheep and quarries, we see, against a hillside of sensual, weathered rock, the remnants of a grand orchard with at least a hundred olive trees, and they're laden with fruit.

'What will happen to these olives?' I ask the owner, leaning on a wooden gate beside her house. Her children ride over on ponies. Dogs bark. Hens and cocks dance our way.

'Some Greeks come up around Easter and take what they can.'

'A carload?'

'Maybe two.'

'Could we pick some as well?'

'Of course.'

Why wasn't everyone clamouring for them? And there

was more good news. The owner told me of another grove further up the road. And there it was, forty more trees. I found the father of the owner under a tractor at the back of a shed.

'Take what you want. We don't use them.'

So we too will have olives for the open day. Real Scone olives. And if the oil's good, there's the possibility of using the old trees for propagation.

Each week, like spies, we examine our secret groves. Are they ripening? Yes. Another heatwave turns the olives at the top of the trees muscat. The colour slowly descends down over the trees like a falling curtain. If they ripen too quickly the birds will get them.

We walk along counting the trees, making notations in the margin of a newspaper. One, two, three, four, slash. One, two, three, four, slash. I start new columns for what seem to be different varieties. They're at least sixty years old and have been battered by the elements and cattle, but their widening trunks show no sign of giving up and the feral trees we've discovered are no doubt their children and grandchildren. Fruit flaunts itself along each unpruned branch, the weight pulling them to the ground. How much fruit is on each tree? We gaze up and guess, then look at each other conceding we've no idea.

I recall a few relevant facts. A good harvest in Tuscany can see one tree yield 80 kilograms, but the average is 50. The Mildura trials have recorded Manzanilla trees with nearly 200 kilograms of fruit per tree. On this basis there has to be a few tonnes ripe for the picking. We prepare to harvest.

A truck delivers fifty orange plastic crates, and ten plastic hand rakes designed to claw at the foliage and bring the olives tumbling down. We wonder how many friends we'll need to hand-pick a tonne. Four people on ladders are meant to be able to harvest a tree in twenty minutes. Four experienced people, that is. Another way of calculating goes like this: one person can pick 120 to 150 kilograms of olives in a day, but if they're inexperienced they're usually so sore afterwards they'll never do it again. Our best hope is to find a group of friends who'll flail around for a few hours between cold drinks and coffee.

Apart from presses great and small, all sorts of gadgets are coming onto the olive market. We're offered a vibrating fork, for example. Some say the shaking, the rippling down the trunk to the roots stimulates growth. Others fear repeated use of such a device will thoroughly depress the tree and make it unproductive. Olive trees can approach the eternal, and I'm deeply adverse to being ruthless. God forbid that we shorten their life expectancy.

We hear of a pecan harvester that was set up for a field day, the claws of which promptly ripped the whole tree out. The operator was apologetic and moved to the next tree. Out that came too. Very embarrassed, he moved to a third. Then gave up.

So we're going to harvest all these trees by hand, aided only by our little hand-held rakes. I gather our team together, make sandwiches, fill eskies, pour coffee into thermos flasks, and scrounge Elmswood for an odd collection of ladders.

Someone once loved these trees, as I'm beginning to love them now. I try to identify the varieties but it isn't easy. One day I'll have this knowledge, take it for granted, but now I lack confidence. Lack knowledge.

I stand beneath the first tree we're going to tackle. Of the tree's fruit, 20% should be green, 60% should be turning red, and the last 20% should be black and fully ripe. This equation, the 20:60:20 that people so often talk about, is the right balance. It gives a high percentage of oil and a high polyphenol count as well. With a low polyphenol count there's the possibility of a briefer shelf life. If the count gets too low, you don't have an extra-virgin oil, what you end up with is a bland yellow liquid fat.

It's a bit like making hay. We have a window of opportunity and it's open right now. We've positioned the ladders, we've spread rolls of shadecloth beneath the trees. The raking and shaking begins. The olives come raining down.

Phillip, JP, Matthew, and friends Nicholas, Gideon, David and Brett are like monkeys in the foliage. David, just back from teaching English in Siberia, is like lightning up and down the ladder. Why can't I do that? After half an hour they decide to modify the hand rakes, binding them to wooden stakes, so that they whack at fruit high above them. The olive boys. Soon the groundsheets are thick with fruit, which I shovel into 20-kilogram crates. But when I try to lift one I fall on my bum.

I ask JP for help. He picks it up easily and plonks it on the truck.

'They want equality,' says JP, 'but they're always asking you to do things for them.'

'You don't look like a farmer, Patrice,' said an old farmer when I hadn't been at Elmswood long. 'Look at your wrists.'

Yes, they're thin, I've always liked their thinness. My wrists could never be mistaken for a man's. I turn them over. Even the hands that used to earn me hundreds of dollars an hour in photographic sessions don't look too bad, thanks to gloves.

But what good are soft hands today?

The team is very, very competitive. Men being men, they're determined to outdo each other. By day's end, everyone is absolutely stuffed but every crate is brimming. Fifty crates by 20 kilograms. We've done it. We've picked a tonne.

We won't sell the oil we press. I just want loads of the stuff to splash over our food and to give away. It's usually so expensive you have to be stingy. I want the freedom to be generous.

Olives Australia has sent out invitations to all and sundry telling them of the open day at Elmswood and the chance to press olives. JP has been tidying up the place and slashing a paddock for parking. The burrs we hadn't got around to chipping are mowed. (If you slash too early they come back like a crop.)

I hear the tractor stop. JP climbs down. He looks at me across the paddock. I know it's bad news from the way he walks towards me. Usually he walks like he talks, slowly, with some awkwardness and reluctance. Today the body language is different.

'The clutch has gone,' he says when he reaches me.

'Gone where?'

'Just gone. Buggered. We'll have to get Wayne over to haul it out.'

We were discussing only the other day how marvellous, touch wood, our 90-horsepower Iseki had been and how we dreaded the expense of a new one. And now with the open day just hours away, it was 'buggered'.

I phone Wayne, who explains what a huge job it is and how it will take days to get the spare parts. Now JP makes matters worse by saying, 'I was going to tell you, the olive press is arriving this afternoon. Andrew reckons we'll need a forklift to get it off. And there aren't any forklifts in Gundy.'

'So what are we going to do?'

'Well, I was going to put the big prongs on the back of the Iseki, the ones we use to lift silage bales.'

'And now the tractor's buggered.'

But we aren't. Charlie, our neighbour, helps out. His tractor is smaller and older but he reckons it can still cope with the silage prongs. After much huffing and puffing he and JP get it in position, but it's a hard tractor to man-oeuvre. When you shift gears it jumps. And while JP is still practising, the truck with the press arrives.

The doors are opened and, lo and behold, it's not a neat little 160-kilogram Oliomio but a 350-kilogram giant. It's twice the weight we expected and beneath its protective plastic wrapping looks very expensive. Which it is, being $17 000 worth.

With the old tractor bucking like a horse at the Gundy rodeo, JP nervously backs it up to the truck and the prongs rise menacingly. Then Demeter, the goddess of harvest, smiles upon us as the prongs slide into the right place on the pallet and the olive press rises like a mighty Wurlitzer. So far so good. But I feel a migraine coming on. It gets worse when I hear shouts, turn around and see JP, who's reversing the tractor up the road, knock down a fence. When he gets to the garage where the pressing is to take place he misses a brick pillar that holds the roof up by a millimetre. A mental note: after we fix the Iseki, let's buy a secondhand forklift.

We're approaching show time. Andrew proudly peels off the plastic and reveals the press. The hundred people who've gathered, some with olives, look appropriately awed. Andrew starts it up. Instead of a low hum it's the sound of a thousand heads banging.

We've reserved the honour of the first pressing. Matthew separates the leaves from the olives in a mechanical sieve, then tips two crates of fruit into a hopper. For an hour nothing can be seen happening, the olives have just disappeared. Then comes the transcendental moment. We stare at a tap as one by one our first drops of olive oil appear – and we've forgotten to position a bucket. Suddenly the garage smells of oil and Italy and all the things I want our grove to be. All eyes are focused on the green stream, now pouring into a stainless-steel container.

Earlier that morning I baked some bread for this occasion. Margaret has cut it into slices and hands it around. One by one, like Catholics at Holy Communion, the congregation comes forward and dips their bread in the oil. It looks and tastes like nothing you buy in the shops. Bright green, fresh, delicious. It's a flavour they've never known.

People are eating more than we can collect. Chins shine with dribbled oil. The olive boys lug more crates. The visitors take it in turn to press their own oil. Everyone is standing around eating, talking, laughing, marvelling – at the machine and the miracle of the oil. In one end go the beads of hope, out the other a liquid food. Throughout the day, and the next two, we keep up a rhythm. Each crate of olives fills another crate with waste. Out the back of the press, purple pulp plops into an old wheelbarrow. And it looks wonderful, as if we should be smearing it onto our faces to cure acne. It has to be good for something, and there's so much of it.

I use our first bottle of oil at dinner. I make polenta in a large salad bowl which I sit on top of a saucepan, cover with foil and stir only three or four times. I charcoal capsicums and eggplants, make pesto, toss salad leaves, toast bread on an open flame, and pour our oil, our first oil, over the lot. We use 700 millilitres for a meal for six.

Phillip's brought back a crate of green olives, probably Verdale, but we're not sure. They were too green for oil. We tried, and out came a liquid you could have poured into an engine. It was almost black, with shades of crimson when we held it up to the sun.

I decide to pickle these green drops, and discover there are many different ways to do it. How much salt is needed? How much water? How often should I change the salt?

Starting off systematically, I sort the bruised fruit. Good this box, bad that box. Rory, dressed in her swimsuit, likes this a lot, but insists we listen to this week's favourite musical, *The Boy from Oz*. She sings along in her attempt at a Peter Allen accent. 'My bay-bear . . . Reeeoh!'

Soon she gives up sorting and starts dancing. She plops some bruised olives into a plastic bottle and I hear the sound of maracas. Now we really are in Rio. They sustain her for hours.

'I love olives, Mum, they make great music.'

Good, darling.

I get bored with sorting olives too, and in the end tip the whole lot, about 50 kilograms, bruised and all, into a big container and pour salty water over them.

JP brings more reject fruit the next day. Every pot is soon filled to overflowing, and I begin to experiment, trying out variations on the pickling theme. I prick some with a fork and slice others, but find it best to be brutal. So I hit them with a hammer, a mallet, anything to bruise them and open them up, then pour a very salty solution over them and keep changing the solution each day for at least two weeks, or until all bitterness has gone. I sterilise jars, fill them with olives, then add more fresh salty water and garlic – or you could use lemon, if you like. Seal.

If you can be bothered to pickle your own, that's my recipe. Tell guests it's Olive Schiacciate when you put them on the table. When I first read about this technique I thought it was crazy. The olives sold in jars or loose at the deli are never smashed. It doesn't sound appealing, but if you don't do this it will take twice, or even three times as long to remove the bitterness, depending on the variety. At least bruise them if you can't take to them with a mallet. This technique won't give you olives to leave on your shelves all year, but it's better to eat up supplies. There's nothing worse than stacking the pantry with this year's apricot jam only to find half a dozen jars from last year hidden behind the chutney.

My mobile rings and a woman asks, 'Are you going to California and Argentina?' I'm standing in the rain, bags of shopping draped over my shoulders as I try to juggle the phone. I open the car door and consider the question.

It's the travel agent and she tells me that Olives Australia is hosting another research trip. Did I know this? Had I seen an application form? Was it lying buried and forgotten on my desk? The travel agent wants a confirmation. Today.

What could I possibly learn about olives in California? They produce the most inedible fruit in the world, as rubbery as car tyres and tasting just as bad. And Argentina's industry isn't much older than ours. Nonetheless I nervously send off a large deposit when I get back to the farm. When I tell Chris Butler I'm going he grunts, 'You've got more money than brains, Patrice.'

So it is a comfort when twenty-five other people sharing the same mental disorder climb on board the tour bus at LA airport a month later. We do a loop of the city before driving 100 kilometres to the Holiday Inn in the desert town of Visalia, a motel with a kidney-shaped swimming pool almost moating the reception desk. I love the smell of chlorine in the morning!

We're in Tulare County, pronounced Ta-Lair-ee. It's October and the landscape is brown. We're below the treeless Sierra Nevada Mountains, travelling in the dust haze caused by harvesting, and being chaperoned by Steve Sibbett from the University of California. The chubby, jovial, mustachioed co-author of *Olive Production Manual*, which many refer to as the olive bible, Steve has spent the last thirty years as a farm adviser, at least in the hours he can spare from eating ribs, drinking beer and fishing.

'Agriculture is a money game,' booms Steve on the bus's microphone. We pass some of the twenty-eight crops grown here in the San Joaquin (pronounced Wa-keen) Valley, worth $3 billion a year. Rows and rows of oranges, grapes, cotton. Channels criss-cross the entire valley, distributing water from the federal dams. This is where hundreds of thousands of Okies, arriving from the dust bowl eighty years ago, were to become white slaves. The area is fenceless, with crops and orchards planted to the road's edge. 'We've killed off all the animals,' says Steve almost proudly. And there's not so much as a bird in sight. Every property we pass is a family operation, the farm their only income. Yet the place looks heartless and industrialised.

As we drive past channel after channel, dam after dam, my hand keeps reaching for my nose, remembering that water represents the dark side of agriculture here. I'm thinking about one of the most memorable moments in the film *Chinatown*, when Roman Polanski puts a knife up Jack Nicholson's nose and slits his nostril. It always bemused me that a leading man could wear a grubby bandage all the way through a film and still retain a glimmer of sex appeal. The story was inspired by the scandal known as the Rape of the Owens Valley; Jack plays a private detective investigating murder and the mysterious disappearance of a vast amount of water.

None of us on the trip has a good word to say about California Black Ripe olives, those deceitfully named dark balls that are artificially made black with a chemical process – a naturally ripened olive cannot be cured and stuffed in a factory without disintegrating. But we are expecting to discover all sorts of high-tech miracles, especially the gadgets they've been developing for harvesting.

A few years back, Phillip and I travelled to Loxton, to one of the oldest groves in South Australia. The new owners, trying to bring the grove back into production after long neglect, were experimenting with a gargantuan shaking machine that gripped the old trunks in a huge crab claw and shook them like castanets. The olives showered out of the trees onto large sheets of canvas, from which they were bundled and poured onto a conveyer belt on its way to a hopper, twigs and leaves lifted en route. The only problem was that the machine was a murderer: we watched as the trunks splintered, and those that weren't ringbarked were all but uprooted.

'Don't worry,' said Phillip, unconvinced, then unconvincingly added, 'I'm sure the machines will be better when we need to buy one in four or five years' time.'

Well, here I am four years later, in the state that gave us *RoboCop*, expecting to see some impressive contraptions, and I'm about to be disappointed. The bus groans up a hill past a few hectares known as hog wallow land – the original, undeveloped landscape where oaks and yuccas dot the hills – until finally we wheeze into an old grove.

Jerry Padula has started harvesting his eight-year-old Manzanillas. Where's the harvester? we wonder as we jump out of the bus. We gaze down the rows at Jerry's harvester – a machine called Mexicans. The despised wetbacks, the legals and the illegals who pour into California, are still out here in the blazing sun. Little has changed since Steinbeck wrote *The Grapes of Wrath*, except now the Okies speak Spanish.

Jerry tried machine harvesting but didn't like it. 'They pulled trees out of the ground. Yah. Snapped off grafts. Yah.' We don't like what we hear. Speaking in a slow, unassuming tone, he sees only a labour-intensive future. 'Yah, we're turning it around. Yah. You know what I mean.' Well, no, we don't actually. And what's with the yahs? Are we on the set of *Fargo*?

Tom Dungan, who owns one of the biggest nurseries in the area, says the days of the small olive grower are over. The two remaining canneries don't even need Californian olives, they can import them more cheaply. No olive grower has made a cent in two years, due to the low prices offered by the canneries. This is something else we don't want to hear. And this year's record crop may well deepen the crisis.

Over the next three days we visit many more groves in Tulare County, mostly planted with Manzanilla, the dual-purpose olive that commands the highest price, or the least lowest, from the canneries. Big crops take longer to harvest, so everyone is nervously behind schedule. We walk through one of the two surviving factories (there used to be twelve) to see how they turn innocent olives into tasteless black tyres before slicing them into treads for the pizza trade. It's heartbreaking seeing so much hard work and energy going into producing such revolting food. At the packing shed, we pass mountains of jars and cans of olives. 'Jumbo', 'Colossal', 'Giant', read the labels. It's got to be big to be good in the US.

Some Tulare County growers, like short, opinionated Italian-American Don Deleonardis, see the future in oil. He's just yanked out his old grove of Manzanillas and planted thirteen thousand Arbequina trees in hedgerows (or, as Michael Burr calls them, fillets) on 8 hectares, and he intends to recruit RoboCop.

Merging with the masses on the freeway, we bypass the capital Sacramento and head for the sleepy town of Corning, which advertises itself as The Olive City. City? Well, the main street stretches for 5 kilometres but it's devoid of any commendable features. Worse, it's devoid of any form of public transport, there's not even a taxi. Yet the blurb on the brochure in the hotel room tells me I've found an ideal vacation getaway. Corning is dreaming of an agri-tourism boom, but it would be easier to push Sisyphus' stone than that idea.

But there's another reason why forgettable Corning imprints itself on my mind: I discover that as well as deceptive marketing, there's such a thing as deceptive planting.

Let's retrace my steps. I'm back home, and can hear the local pop station blasting from JP's white Toyota parked up on the hill. (He knows how much I hate it, but he isn't expecting to see me this morning.) I need to tell him something, so I head towards him through the new plantings. Soon the pop station yields to the sound of his slow, melodic whistle. He looks up, startled by my approach. Although I've seen him almost every day for thirteen years, I'm always surprised by the open Australianness of JP's face. He's always busy but never rushing, unlike anyone I knew in Sydney. JP's job is diverse, demanding and unpredictable. He is so multiskilled it's hard to describe and measure, and he has a quality which is on the decline: he actively listens. He's in the process of restaking one of the olive trees, which looks like it's been knocked by an animal. We'd been cursing kangaroos until we realised we had feral pigs visiting as well, I'd even found their diggings in the garden. JP kept banging at the stake until I was standing, puffing and breathless, beside him. He smiled. He wanted to talk. But I told him I hadn't come up for a chat, just to tell him that the cattle truck was coming an hour earlier. He pushed the point and said, slightly peeved, 'It won't hurt to have a look at this tree together.' He was right. I hadn't been looking at the trees much, too depressing.

'Come over here.' He walked me down to the end of a row that curved around the hill. 'You get a good indication of it here.'

'Of what?'

'These trees are not all the same.'

It was as clear as that. There was no denying it, the difference was unequivocal. They'd appeared identical when we planted them as long, leafy stems, but now many trees were a lighter shade of grey-green. They were all meant to be Correggiola, a tree with a relaxed, bushy shape, whereas many of these were upright, as if standing at attention, their arms giving the fascist salute to Mussolini.

Julian from Olives Australia would visit a few weeks later and admit there was a problem, that they may have mixed up some varieties, and yes, he'd had complaints from other growers. DNA tests were underway, but it's a long, slow process to establish the genetic makeup of an olive tree. I tried to remain calm about it; after all, the ring-ins might end up being a top-class oil variety rather than the miserable pickling type I feared.

Now here I am with Julian at Corning, heading for a Tex-Mex joint for dinner. Over plates of sloppy food I learn that not only are many of our Correggiola trees not Correggiola, but the five hundred Mission we've planted are in fact Manzanilla.

Thirty-something, Julian is a handsome, fit vegetarian with a constantly beaming smile. His white teeth dazzle.

His eyes twinkle. His friends tell me that once you know him you can tell when it's a stressed smile hiding frustration and tiredness, or a genuine expression of happiness and goodwill. Tonight I sense a man just managing with his lot. For a start he's missing his wife Melinda and their one-year-old Ethan. 'Ethan gets his first tooth and I'm not there. He takes his first crawl and I'm not there. He takes his first step, I'm not there.' I know where he'd rather be right now and it's not sitting in a Tex-Mex joint in Corning with me. But here we are anyway.

'The Mission we sent out weren't Mission,' he tells me. 'They're all Manzanilla, Patrice. All of them.'

'What?' This chilli is too hot. I must be hearing things.

I'll never forget the look on Julian's face, reacting to the look on mine. 'I thought you already knew,' he says. This bad news turns out to be old news. A letter explaining the latest DNA findings was sent out to all customers days before we left, but for some reason our mail was late. This is the first I've heard of it. A few mismatched trees among the Correggiola I could live with, but an entire section covering 2 hectares is a disaster. Even worse, the trees are the dreaded Manzanilla, which many growers regard as no better than weeds. Only the day before, we met growers pulling them out and replanting with Arbequina. Mission versus Manzanilla. It's like coming home from the maternity ward with the wrong baby.

Hundreds of wrong, wrong, wrong trees. I feel angry.

I feel sick. I can't look Julian in his beaming, handsome face. I just want to cry.

Had I been home reading the circular letter, I'd have been on the phone in an instant, shouting, but here in this cheap diner, with Julian opposite me sensing my despair, almost crying himself, I don't know what to do. Or what to say.

'Oh Julian, Julian,' I say finally. 'This is one hell of a stuff-up.'

Later I'd learn that other nurseries had made similar mistakes, but how on earth could Olives Australia, the company that had started this frenzy of planting in the 1990s and had profited the most from this renaissance, have sold countless thousands of the wrong trees?

And it would get worse. The variety known unromantically as UC13A6 turned out to be Manzanilla as well. And Australia's Pendulina wasn't matching Pendolino at the research institute in Spain. Chris Butler would make the point that the Australian olive industry was far from being an industry at all, but was still based on the nursery. And he warned that it would be hard to survive without certified trees.

We were dealing with honest mistakes. There was no malicious intent, no conspiracy to make money at the expense of gullible olive growers. Nor had Olives Australia guaranteed the varieties they sold and, in a day and age of class actions, it was hard to blame them.

But now, with growers discovering the magnitude of the mess, a circular letter of apology isn't good enough. Not that Julian needs reminding. Along with Michael Burr he is a member of the cumbersomely titled National Olive Variety Determination and Improvement Board (its acronym NOVDIB sounding like a leftover from the Soviet Union), whose job it is to verify varieties in Australia. They clearly have a huge job ahead of them.

'We've been selling varieties to the best of our under-standing,' says Julian. 'Unless there's computer tracking and double tagging on every tree, mistakes will be made.'

'And have been,' I say.

Years ago you identified trees simply by looking at them. If it looked like a chook, acted like a chook, clucked like a chook, the chances were it was a chook. But the advent of DNA fingerprinting, which helps enormously in sorting out some synonyms and antonyms, doesn't put definition beyond argument.

As we walk back to the motel, Julian says, 'Imagine you're in the stud business selling Herefords. Let's say you'd bought your original stock from a big-time stud. You've the papers to prove it. But new tests reveal that your animals are actually Devons. It's just that they *look* like Herefords. Over the years, there's been an evolutionary change, but no one's ever noticed. Then the DNA reveals the truth. Same with olives.'

Olive trees propagated by cuttings will have the same

genetic makeup (genotype) as the original tree. But there may well be subtle changes, and occasionally massive changes, in appearance when the trees are grown in different environments. A variety has traditionally been just a group of trees that look similar. So errors in labelling are compounded. The so-called old mother plots, seventy trees at Stoneville Research Station in Western Australia, along with many more under scrutiny at Wagga Wagga and Mildura, have been the foundation of Australia's gene pool. Unfortunately, some of these mother plot trees were labelled incorrectly, leading us into confusion. It's a bit like the time measurements at Greenwich being slightly out of whack.

I've always believed that when the industry develops we'll be selling varietal oils, just as our Hunter Valley neighbours sell varietal wines. And undoubtedly the confusions of early plantings will force us to have our varieties certified.

The next day, back on the bus, I ask my fellow travellers what they know about the variety debacle. Most have read the circular. Some have planted different varieties and so are unaffected. Some, like me, are still confused and angry.

Poor Susan Sweeney. Sitting beside me, she had to endure my wrath for the next few days. The Development Officer (Olives) for the Primary Industries Department in South Australia, Susan has been co-ordinating another mysterious acronym, NOVA: the National Olive Variety

Assessment program. A small serious energetic scientist, Susan is, believe it or not, one of only two people paid by any tier of government to do focused research on olives. Even more incredible is the fact that her funding has a sunset clause – she doesn't have enough time to complete half of the project she's overseeing.

In 1997 I'd filled out a NOVA questionnaire detailing what we'd planted, or what we thought we'd planted. Information from growers across the nation was to be fed into a database to create a long-term assessment of tree performance. Nothing could be more important. Susan Sweeney had phoned to arrange a visit to Elmswood but the dreaded frost had just laid waste to the grove. 'There's no point coming,' I said. 'They're *all* dead.' So she was surprised to see me on the trip. Why would the curator of a tree cemetery be interested in California's olive industry?

We, the guinea pigs, need to have our experiences collated and compared. Of course the raw data is years away from being any use to me, but some lucky people, yet to be born perhaps, will be the beneficiaries. It's what our fledgling industry could give to the future – the opportunity to learn from our mistakes. Mistakes like planting misidentified trees.

At Corning the farmers are doing it hard. Instead of worrying about varieties they're wondering whether it's worthwhile having olive trees at all. The canneries have just posted their price list for the season, and things are looking grimmer than ever.

Most locals run mixed farms, with almonds and prunes to improve their income. They douse their orchards with artificial fertiliser, and use chemicals in a process called chemical thinning, whereby the whole tree is sprayed to make some of the fruit fall off. Their intention is to have the right amount of fruit mature at the right time, at the right size, because fruit that looks right is the easiest to sell. But if the weather changes, or they spray a little too much, *all* the fruit can fall off. The chemical dependence at Corning is total and there's no interest in reducing it, let alone eliminating the addiction. I find only one processor with a boutique organic grove, but the motivation is purely market-driven, not environmental.

We glimpse teams of Mexican pickers moving amongst the trees everywhere we go. 'Mexican labourers are becoming Americanised,' grumbles a grower. 'Last year I had a hundred of them standing right here telling me they wanted 50 cents more per box. They knew we were short of pickers.'

Matt Koball manages some of the Mexican teams. He and his wife Ann used to work in the space industry, but left to grow olives. We can all identify with that: leave a perfectly sound, high-paying job, and farm. Finding it difficult to make a living, Ann took a job with Hewlett Packard to help the paranoid prepare for Y2K, while Matt began networking with the Mexicans to co-ordinate their efforts and prevent exploitation. There are old buildings on their property to accommodate workers, and for half the year a hundred Mexicans live in, ready for picking or pruning contracts.

Eventually we see a mechanical harvester displaying its questionable robotic skills. Big diesel monsters are getting some fruit off the trees, but every machine is experiencing problems: if the fruit is green, it won't shake off; if the ground is wet, the monsters get bogged; if the trees aren't pruned appropriately, up to 40% of the fruit gets left on the branches. Reluctant to commit to the technology, farmers are trying it out on parts of their orchards, but are quickly learning that saving on Mexicans usually means damaging trees.

From Corning we head north to Sonoma and Napa Counties, in the heartland of the Californian wine industry. We talk of an explosion of grape planting in Australia – here it's positively nuclear. A local joke is that if you leave soil in the back of your truck for long, someone will plant grapes in it.

It's here I meet my first kindred spirits, Jeffrey and Anne-Marie Allen, organic farmers committed to environmental issues and a life devoid of polluting junk. They've been recruited to show us around Healdsburg, an area reminiscent of Possum Creek behind Byron Bay. It's drop-dead pretty, but you cannot escape the distant hum of the freeway. We stop at Ridgely Ever's 9-hectare grove to see the trees that make DaVero Dry Creek Olive Oil, one of the better known Californian boutique brands. Having invested hundreds of thousands of dollars in land (prices here range from $35 000 to $40 000 an acre, twenty times more than our area), Ridgely knows how hard it is to profit from olive oil when, as he says, you can plant corn in May and get corn oil in September. 'So the only way to earn money from olives is to go the gold-label, gold-medal route, be very exclusive and charge huge prices.'

On to Glen Ellen, famed for its association with Jack London (Wolf House was just around the hill). In the middle of the town, at the end of a cluster of wooden buildings on a tourist strip and at the back of a little shop full of olive-related souvenirs, we find The Olive Press, an elegant processing plant. Through a thick glass wall, customers can watch olives being pressed, the oil bottled to order. For two days each year the owners conduct a community pressing, where anyone with any amount of olives can bring their fruit.

In Marin County there's a stone-mill press behind glass, used as a drawcard for the restaurant Il Frantoio, the brain-child of Robert Zecca, a former banker who spends half the year at his thousand-year-old Tuscan villa and the other watching the cash register ring at his successful eatery.

But a few brave experiments do not make an industry. From the San Joaquin Valley to Sonoma County, it becomes clear that California provides no shining example for Australia to follow. In the south it's as stifled by tradition as Spain and Italy. In the north it's driven by gourmet wankery.

Will things be better in Argentina?

When I told people I was going to Argentina, their faces lit up. They thought tango, macho, gaucho, the Paris of the south, Madonna (not Evita). I thought a country wasted by corruption, dictatorships, thirty thousand 'disappeared', the Islas Malvinas, Nazi exiles, and haunting memories of the film *The Official Story*, directed by Luis Puenzo, about a middle-class woman who cannot have a child. Her husband arranges an adoption, but then she discovers the child is stolen. An argument ensues, her hand slips between the opening of a door, below the hinges, and the husband, pushing the door shut, breaks her fingers. I can still feel it, hear the crunch. This act of violence seemed to sum up what I thought and feared about Argentina. It's an uneasy place.

Seven relentless days have been organised. We fly into Buenos Aires, climb onto a bus, and are denied a brief tour of the city by a political rally. Or rather, the bus driver thinks that's the problem as we inch our way through noisy, ugly streets for three hours, arriving at the domestic airport with just seconds to spare.

Our schedule will take us through the northern provinces of Catamarca, La Rioja, San Juan, Mendoza, all on the eastern side of the Andes, areas well and truly outside the tourist loop. It's as if we've arrived in Australia only to visit Roma, Mt Isa and Katherine. Argentina, second in size in South America after Brazil, has a population twice that of

Australia. We find ourselves in an area of 25% unemployment, poverty, and a lack of essential services. The tourist guides are right to describe it as undeveloped. If Buenos Aires is the Paris of the south, this is more like Algeria.

But just as our beef competes with Argentine beef, our olive oil is destined, perhaps doomed, to compete as well. Far from spontaneously resurrecting, like ours, their olive industry is partially planned by government. The official objective is to provide jobs in struggling provinces and earn pesos from exports rather than import replacement. They intend planting 40 000 hectares of olives. At three hundred and thirty trees per hectare, that's 13.2 million trees. At last count in 1999, 12 000 hectares were under cultivation.

All this activity has come about because of a tax deferral scheme that's been underway for a decade. If a company wishes to delay paying a hefty tax bill, they can invest in orchards in these arid provinces and be granted 100% deferral for ten years. Then they have another six years to satisfy the Tax Office. On more than one occasion we hear unfunny jokes about another junta taking over so there'll be no need to pay back the tax at all. Others snigger about drug money being laundered by the orchards.

But the scheme doesn't necessarily make the deserts bloom. Whilst millions of pesos are pouring into the area and much of the landscape is transformed, we still see the odd thousand-hectare failed vineyard, overgrown with creepers and utterly deserted. Jojoba was the first crop of choice, then wine grapes, which make up most of the planting. Now olives. Can olives, innocent olives, salvage rural Argentina? On both sides of the Pacific, we're burdening the boughs of the olive tree with a lot of responsibility.

There's one road in and out of Catamarca. It might be a shabby, unfinished town without much civic pride, but it has a noisy chaotic charm and the people are happy. Even the dogs lying about in endless siesta seem to smile. The town rests between two mountain ranges, Sierra Ambato at 2200 metres and Sierra Ancasti at 1600 metres. High by Australian standards, their summits are merely the foothills of the Andes. Four hundred millimetres of rain are dumped here in December and January, leaving the rest of the year in drought, but the melting snows keep the water flowing for town and agriculture.

Our bus takes us down the main road, through a mix of smog and dust haze. All the new agribusinesses are set up along this main road. Left to itself, the desert landscape is like Nevada's, filled with cacti of various sorts – tall phallic forms and squat prickly-pear types punctuated by spiky shrubs and tufts of grass. But dozers are pushing this all aside to make way for groves. The soil is pure sand, it could have come from Bondi.

The first grove we visit, a massive 800 hectares, is owned by the Romero family, newspaper proprietors in Salta who obviously have a big tax problem. I'm reminded of home by the windbreaks of she-oaks, the same *Casuarina cunninghamiana* that line our river, and remember the way we marvelled at our few thousand trees when we discussed the complexities of grove management. Here I'm overwhelmed by the scale of the enterprise. I stand next to a four-year-old tree in the middle of a grove, rows radiating in every direction, disappearing into the haze, and don't know whether I want to applaud or bawl. On the one hand, you can't help but think how clever humans are, turning sand into salads, simplifying procedures until sixty people can look after 800 hectares. But, on the other hand, I deplore this kind of mechanised agriculture that takes the soul out of growing things. The innate satisfaction that comes from growing things yourself is dying. Somehow even the cacti feel more friendly.

These ventures are meant to provide job opportunities for the locals, and no one can criticise that, but with wages at $US2 an hour, or $US18 a day, the distribution of that tax deferral money isn't particularly equitable. A beer still costs the same in Catamarca as it does in Gundy. The local people here aren't the owners of the Argentine olive industry, they're just the serfs.

I'm irritated by the observations of a fellow traveller: 'This is the way to do it. Lucky devils too, they have what we'll never have, cheap labour.'

Day passes day and it's a blur of huge and identical operations. Tired of endless perspectives of trees, I focus on the sign behind the driver's seat, EVITEMOS EL COLERA – 'Prevent cholera'. Maybe agribusiness isn't the only contagious disease raging below the Andes. My travel guide has a map ostensibly showing the danger areas in South America, but it's hard to work out the coding. Are black areas bad, or the white areas? I pass the map around and we reach consensus that we're in the middle of a cholera black zone. And now everyone is reading the sign behind the driver, who offers us water from a container that suddenly none of us wants to drink. Will the ice I ordered last night for my vodka and orange juice kill me?

I hate to admit it, but on first impression the trees in these mega-groves look healthy. The soil, or rather the sand, is sprayed regularly with herbicide, so the only things allowed to flourish are the olives. The growers practise fertigation – the adding of fertiliser to the water which is pumped from stations the size of houses. And they pump often because sand is lacking in elements.

Yet we notice something odd. It is spring and we're looking at trees that are three and four years old but there isn't a single olive to be seen. In Australia even very young trees have a few olives dangling, but here there isn't one. These trees – a mixture of Arbequina, Frantoio, Leccino, Fargo, and Manzanilla – are meant to grow a metre a year. Perhaps pushing them with so much fertiliser has been counterproductive? Or is it the ferocious winds? Perhaps they've blown away the blossoms?

We stop at La Veloz (The Fast), a spectacular grove 75 kilometres south of Catamarca. Here the manager, the gorgeous Guillermo, he of the piercing green eyes, gives us the run-down on the 400 hectares already planted. Out come satellite photographs from 1985 and 1999 showing the transformation in the valley. The site was chosen because the winds allegedly aren't so bad. It's the closest grove to the Andes and they're planting right up the slopes, yet are worried about causing mud-slides when the rains come around Christmas. Insanely, the planners consider this a risk worth taking. Not even the sloppiest, most pro-development council in Australia would have dared issue an approval.

After lunch, a battle to the death with tough Argentine beef, we cluster around Guillermo holding our hats to our heads as the winds blow his words away. Later, when we can hear him, he tells us it isn't a particularly blowy day.

And the wind may be the least of their problems. Moving along the valley we see a 5000-hectare grove that has lost 3000 hectares of trees to frost. It makes my grieving over six hundred frostbitten saplings seem excessive. And it's chilling to realise that the temperature range in Gundy is far wider; we dip below their minus 3 degrees and soar above 39. But not, of course, in the same day.

The term of President Menem, he of the weird hair, is almost over when we arrive in La Rioja province, an area known as the cradle of the olive industry. It's described in California as the only region where olives can succeed in

Argentina. There's great scepticism in the US about the vast Argentianian experiment, but here, around the town of Aimogasta, it's conceded that the climate seems just perfect. We're invited into an airconditioned tasting room to a repast of olives, cheese, Coke and Sprite, but I'm delighted to see that the traditional methods of processing prevail.

Aimogasta is the home of the big juicy Arauco olive, the only acknowledged Argentine variety. Three hundred years ago, the story goes, the King of Spain ordered Argentina's olive trees be cut down because they were posing a threat to Spain's domestic industry. But a lone Indian woman from the Diaguitas tribe loved her Arauco olive tree so much she risked her life to save it. Today this tree, called the father of the Arauco (why not the mother?) produces 500 kilograms of fruit per year, and is an object of veneration and a tourist attraction. It's the oldest and largest olive tree we've ever seen. As gnarled as a mallee root, painted white for protection, it takes eight of us holding hands to surround its trunk.

Back on the bus I fall asleep.

'Patrice? Patrice? Are you asleep?' says Andrew.

'I was.'

'I thought you were. Your eyes were shut.'

'Thanks for telling me.'

Massive groves need massive processing plants. Next on our agenda is a two-storey extravaganza with mezzanine offices, a tasting room, and temperature-controlled storage capable of holding millions of litres of oil. There is nothing like it anywhere else in the world, but our tour guide is reluctant to give us the tour. We've arrived as Argentina is about to kick off in a World Cup rugby match with Ireland. We are brushed aside as he heads to a television set. Later we recuperate at a bistro on the Plaza de Mayo, but it's hard to get the attention of the waiter, all of Argentina is watching its heroes on television.

Big as Argentine groves are, they're going to get bigger. The consensus is that the businesses will merge and monopolise so as to achieve the economies of scale deemed necessary for world conquest. That's why the Argentine industry shows no interest in visiting Australia. Although there's been a long tradition of olive growing in Argentina, olive oil consumption is only 180 millilitres per person per year (in Australia it's a litre per person per year, and in Spain it's 12 litres). All these trees, all these processing plants are to make an export product. Presently most of the produce is being sold to Brazil, within the MERCOSUR trading block, which encompasses Brazil, Argentina, Uruguay and Paraguay. And if the scale of the groves, processing plants, cheap labour and tax deferrals, not to mention an import levy, isn't bad enough, we learn that the current wholesale price for oil is $2 a litre, a fraction of Australian production costs.

Sitting in front of his EVITEMOS EL COLERA sign (we found out there is no cholera in Argentina), our bus driver has a reassuring resemblance to Merv Hughes. And he's drinking an appropriately named beverage, called *maté*. It's a thick green tea, made from the *yerba maté* plant, which most Argentines seem to be addicted to, and he's sucking it through a tube stuck into something that looks like a bong. It's hot outside and Merv tells us that the airconditioning has broken down (though the next driver will have no trouble turning it on). More seriously, it's now getting dark and the headlights don't work, or he doesn't know how to turn them on either. Fortunately a three-quarter moon rises above the Andes to light our way to the beautiful city of Mendoza. Though built on canals, it's more famous for its tree-lined streets. We're proudly told that there are eight hundred thousand trees, one for every person. They're so closely planted that, as the bus drives towards the hotel, the roof is battered by branches.

Seventy percent of Argentina's wine is produced here. Wherever there's wine, there are always olives. At one winery, an old traditional oil press is displayed in the courtyard. An Argentine woman, brown and blonde with a defiant fuck-you attitude, takes us through the dos and don'ts of wine and oil tasting. At the end of her spiel, Andrew hands her a small gift and she says, 'Thank you, because you know how to do it for me!'

'That's what I want,' one Aussie processor says. 'A few really good-looking chicks handing around olives.'

Sitting in a cafe in the mall at Mendoza later that night,

we notice the place is full of foreigners. But they're not tourists or people on a business tour, they're all part of an influx of expertise. Some are engineers, some are in information technology, others are teachers. One woman turns to us and fixing her eyes on Andrew, says, 'I've been here for months and I have generated *no* interest in anybody.' She goes on to explain that it's all a big front with Argentine men. Her friend focuses on Bruce. Realising that we're surplus to requirement, Susan Sweeney and I walk home, wending our way through the eight hundred thousand trees.

There's bedlam next morning at breakfast. Having phoned home, one of the team announces that Jeff Kennett is out. Shock. Disbelief. Joy. Despair. I get an English-language Argentine newspaper (Kennett doesn't get a mention) and read that Gusmao has returned to East Timor, that the Australian republican headquarters has had its database attacked. Half a page is devoted to Steve Waugh and cricket.

On the last day we meet one of the nobility of the Argentine industry, the distinguished vigneron and olive producer Enrique Tittarelli, who I'm pleased to see has donkeys roaming the property, just like we do at home. Señor Tittarelli says he will teach the masses to love olive oil, convinced that education is the missing link.

Formal gardens surround the original farmhouse built by his grandfather, now used for lectures. We're to attend one on matters organoleptic.

'Nature is a good maker of oil,' says Señor Tittarelli, illuminated by the slide projector light. 'Man can ruin it!'

His attention to detail is impressive. Unfortunately, most of us haven't been tasting oils for very long and much of his passionate intensity is lost in translation. (Translators should be required to have mellifluous voices, ours doesn't.) Nonetheless, it is loud and clear that the appreciation of flavour is a lifetime pursuit. Much time must be dedicated to tastings, Señor Tittarelli intones. And then changing the subject, 'Late harvest is a crime!' We taste and spit a less than perfect oil caused by this avoidable mishap. As we put the last cup aside, the señor expresses anxiety about all the new plantings. 'The scale of it all!' His eyes roll to heaven. 'Quantity is replacing quality.'

From every bus stop, wall, shopfront, and viaduct, Eduardo De La Rua's aristocratic face stares at us. He's surrounded by images of other contesting politicians. Tomorrow the nation will go to the polls. Our inept translator has been recruited to aid the electoral process. He manages to warn us that from midnight tonight, no alcohol will be sold. Indeed many places won't open this evening. Having missed out on restaurants and clubs all week because Argentines dine at 10pm and don't start dancing until after midnight, we've been looking forward to some free time and conviviality. Now the doors will be closed against us. Finally we find a restaurant-cabaret that somewhat reluctantly lets us in. It's 8pm, we're the only guests, and the menu is limited to steak and chicken.

When we left Australia we were looking forward to the flavour of famous Argentine beef. But in ten days we never find it. Every day one host or another barbecues round, topside or brisket of beef, and cuts it into big rough cubes. Invariably it is well done, often overdone. Tonight my steak is a thin triangle of unknown origin that deflects the fork and rejects the knife. I try desperately to hold it in place so I can apply more force with the knife's worn serration, but it doesn't work. I lean over to Marcello, an Argentine olive consultant, and ask him to tell the waiter that there's an old boot on my plate. He conveys the essence of the message somewhat more diplomatically. I give the waiter a demonstration of the problem and he suggests I try another knife. Then another and another and another. Five knives later, I give up, and so does the waiter. I tell Marcello not to worry, I wasn't really hungry anyway.

Do we have to go to a five-star restaurant to taste the good stuff? If so, then what's the point? Anyone can get top food in a top place. In our experience Argentina's beef doesn't deserve its reputation – the food writers must always be eating in places with Michelin ratings. I'm longing for some Elmswood beef. If the Argentines are as good at mythologising their oil as they are their meat, we'll be in even bigger trouble.

The band starts up, performers take the stage, and

dancers the floor. And here's another disappointment: no tango. It turns out that this most famous and passionate of dances is exclusive to Buenos Aires, and perhaps to five-star cabarets.

Next morning we leave Mendoza, passing between oil wells – petroleum, not olive – and follow the brown Mendoza river upstream to the Andes. An hour later we find ourselves where *Seven Years in Tibet* was filmed. The road winds above the river, beside a deserted train track. The entire railway system was closed in 1978 when conflict and mismanagement in the junta led to its dereliction. Now its sad, rusted remains are being covered with rock falls, and soon it will become another ancient ruin along the way. Centuries-old stone houses cluster here and there, all but indistinguishable from the weathered rock and debris. Perhaps archaeological digs in the future will confuse the railways with the pre-Columbian era, and marvel at the abilities of the ancients to run steam trains. Our road, a single lane each way, is the only route from Mendoza to Chile. We're travelling too fast, leaning into the person beside us as we round the bends. The men who know about such things agree that the sound of the revving is wrong, that the driver is using the wrong gear. Making matters worse, the driver shouts back at us telling us of the many accidents along the road, and, lo and behold, we start seeing bits of vehicles lodged in crevasses in the cliffs or scattered down the precipices. But we survive, reaching the snow level, and if the clouds were more considerate, we'd be able to see the 6962-metre Cerro Aconcagua, South America's highest peak. Chile is just down the road.

We stretch our legs at Puente del Inca, where a natural stone bridge arches over the Mendoza River, and breathe the thin, icy air. Warned that the altitude will exhaust us, I step down from the bus at the border and can hardly stand up. This surely is why drug taking is referred to as a high. The light-headedness isn't altogether unpleasant, but unfortunately doesn't last long. Our introduction to Chile is to wind down a stretch of road infamous for its twenty-three hairpin turns without a safety guard in sight. We're travelling fast enough, but buses and petrol tankers zoom by, slewing on the curves, their drivers still enjoying the high. Who needs Disneyland? Thank heavens we haven't had lunch. It's been a long time since, as a little girl in Adelaide, I've prayed, but I pray this day. Down in the valley, amongst the vineyards of Chile, I look back at the Andes that have taken seven hours to cross, and already I want to go back.

It rained every week while I was away and now the garden is a jungle, teeming with life. Albertine, the prolific climbing rose that drapes the garage, is in full bloom and the scent of lavender fills the air. I'm not quite ready to walk amongst our olives, but can see the grove willowing in the wind down by the river. But first, a cup of tea.

When away from the farm I think about it all the time. I look forward to a break, but when I get one my mind never leaves Elmswood. Free of boring lists of what has to be done, bills to be paid, plantings, pipes and broken machines, and free too of flies, mosquitoes and heat, my mind fills with moods and memories, usually autumnal. I see how parts of the property have changed during our short time here. How the river takes a different course after every flood, filling old waterholes and providing new ones, sculpting a new sandy bank or redesigning a little island. Time away is precious, allowing ideas to be sealed into the soul.

Before sunset, holding hands, the three of us, Phillip, Rory and I, set out for a long stroll, noisily attended by Molly and Rosie. As we near the shearing shed I see that Phillip has conscientiously slashed the grass between the rows with the Kuboto. It's like lawn, even and neat. An inviting pathway. Many trees died here, even though we planted after the frosts. Then came the hares (and at this instant Molly and Rosie spot one and head off in pursuit), and then we didn't water enough during a heatwave. A winter deluge bogged others and slowly their leaves folded, yellowing in disgust.

But time has been healing. Instead of counting the missing, I celebrate the strength of the survivors. These are the tough ones. Our future breeders. We'll take cuttings next autumn and plant out their offspring. Ours is a grove where each tree retains its individuality, unlike the endless stretches of trees being mechanically pruned in Argentina and California.

JP spots us and joins us and begins telling stories about specific trees, just as he does about specific cattle. 'Remember how the pigs knocked this one down? And then the cockatoos nipped off the main trunk? But the new growth has been good.' Or, 'There was a leak here in the pipe and these two trees were overwatered and you can still see that the leaves are a slightly different colour.' Our grove feels like an extended family, for our extended family.

Olives and oil will continue to be consumed, but the survival of the olive as a tree is less certain. As the new century gains pace and we accelerate our already fast lives, the olive tree will most likely be manipulated, genetically engineered into a shrub and planted as a hedge so that machines can more efficiently pick the fruit. A hillside of olives could resemble a vineyard. And eventually the genetic engineers may be able to produce an olive without a tree at all. Just as they threaten to produce steak without an animal.

The olive tree may live on only in neglected groves and gardens around the world. To be recalled on Greek vases, on the tombs of ancient Egypt, in the poetry and literature of history, in the legend of Noah's Ark, in images like Picasso's peace dove.

It is the olive, as a tree, that we plant at Elmswood. And I can hardly wait to grow old with them.

ACKNOWLEDGEMENTS

Had Anna Maria Monticelli not arranged a meeting with her ex-husband, the assistant news director at Channel 7, I wouldn't have been offered a job as a researcher. And if I hadn't investigated chemical pollution for one of Kerry O'Brien's documentaries, I wouldn't have discovered biodynamics. Telling just part of the story at Elmswood, the book neglects to thank the many who've mustered, shorn, fenced, repaired, ploughed, weeded, and helped in so many ways. And I haven't paid tribute to the friends, especially the many members of the olive fraternity, who were there to encourage me when the dramas and dilemmas became overwhelming.

I'm grateful to biodynamic farmers across Australia, the unsung heroes of our agriculture whose determination to keep alive the art of farming, to trust their own instincts, to be actively perceptive, were and remain inspirational. Particular thanks go to David Marks and Heidi Fallding.

Having read an early draft, Elizabeth Bullen was a great sounding board. Rebecca Adams' constant encouragement and Gail Cork's willingness to answer questions grammatical are deeply appreciated. Una Price of the Scone and Upper Hunter Historical Society was generous with her time, finding references and phone numbers and patiently photocopying documents.

I couldn't have coped without Elmswood's manager, JP.

We usually call him Phil, but due to the confusion with Phillip he had to be rechristened for the book. Together with his son Matthew, Phil kept Elmswood on course whenever I was absent from the bridge.

Thanks to Meredith Rose at Penguin for her conscientious editing. And Julie Gibbs, Executive Publisher at Penguin, who thought the idea was good from the outset.

Most of all, I want to thank Phillip and Rory, who shared it all.

Grateful acknowledgement is due to the following for permission to quote from their published works: Faber and Faber for the extract on page 57 from T.S. Eliot's poem 'The Hollow Men' (*Collected Poems 1909–1962*, London, 1963), and for the extract on page 207 from Lawrence Durrell's *Prospero's Cell* (London, 1945); Duffy & Snellgrove for the extract on page 86 from Robert Gray's poem 'Currawongs', first published in *Lineations* (Sydney, 1996) and now in print in *New Selected Poems* (Sydney, 1998); Penguin UK and the estate of Elizabeth David for the extract on page 208 from Elizabeth David's *A Book of Mediterranean Food* (London, 1950).

The lyrics from *Kismet*, on pages 202–3, are reproduced by permission of Warner/Chappell Music Australia Pty Ltd.